Fr. Robert J. Kus

FLOWERS IN THE WIND 6

More Story~Based Homilies for Cycle C

RED LANTERN PRESS
WILMINGTON, NORTH CAROLINA

www.redlanternpress.com

Publications of Red Lantern Press

Journals by Fr. Robert J. Kus

- Dreams for the Vineyard: Journal of a Parish Priest – 2002

- For Where Your Treasure Is: Journal of a Parish Priest – 2003

- There Will Your Heart Be Also: Journal of a Parish Priest – 2004

- Field of Plenty: Journal of a Parish Priest – 2005

- Called to the Coast: Journal of a Parish Priest – 2006

- Then Along Came Marcelino: Journal of a Parish Priest – 2007

- Living the Dream: Journal of a Parish Priest – 2008

- A Hand to Honduras: Journal of a Parish Priest – 2009

- Beacon of Hope: Journal of a Parish Priest – 2010

- Serving God By Serving Others: Journal of a Parish Priest – 2011

Homily Collections by Fr. Robert J. Kus

- Flowers in the Wind 1 – Story-Based Homilies for Cycle B

- Flowers in the Wind 2 – Story-Based Homilies for Cycle C

- Flowers in the Wind 3 – Story-Based Homilies for Cycle A

- Flowers in the Wind 4 – More Story-Based Homilies for Cycle A

- Flowers in the Wind 5 – More Story-Based Homilies for Cycle B

- Flowers in the Wind 6 – More Story-Based Homilies for Cycle C

Dedication

In Loving Memory of

My Uncle and Aunt

Jim and Bobbie Bush

Of

Stow, Ohio

Acknowledgements

Many thanks go to Nolan Heath and Pat Marriott of the Basilica Shrine of St. Mary in Wilmington, N.C. who helped with the editing of these homilies.

Many thanks also go to the parishioners of both St. Catherine of Siena Parish in Wake Forest, N.C. and the Basilica Shrine of St. Mary for whom I originally created these homilies.

Table of Contents

Introduction

TABLE OF CONTENTS

Introduction

The purpose of this book is to provide Catholic preachers a complete second collection of Sunday (& Christmas) homilies for Cycle C. Though it is designed specifically for Catholic priests and deacons, the homilies should prove useful for preachers in other mainstream Christian denominations as well.

Each homily starts with the Sunday of the Year being celebrated followed by the Scripture selection that is being discussed. This is followed by a story that appeals for people of all ages. Finally, each homily then discusses the concepts that can be gleaned from the Scripture and story and how we can apply them to our everyday lives.

Each homily takes less than eight minutes. This is especially important for preachers who are in parishes that have Masses every 90 minutes and have to get parking lots filled and emptied in a limited amount of time.

The homilies were created while I was pastor of parishes with large concentrations of children. I'm happy to say the stories make the homilies vibrant and interesting, and families love talking about the stories during the week.

Preachers may take the homilies whole, or they may tweak them to fit their specific needs.

Every effort has been made to credit the authors of each story. In the event that this was not possible, the story sources are listed as being written by "Anonymous."

Part One

ADVENT &
CHRISTMAS SEASONS

Chapter 1

1ˢᵗ Sunday of Advent - C
The Dilbert Story

***

Scripture:

- Jeremiah 33: 14-16
- Psalm 25: 4-5, 8-9; 10 & 14
- 1 Thessalonians 3: 12 - 4: 2
- Luke 21: 25-28, 34-36

Today we begin a new Church Year, Year C, the Year of St. Luke. That means that for the most part, each week when we come to celebrate the Sunday Eucharist, we'll be hearing from the Gospel of St. Luke.

We begin new Church Years with the Season of Advent, a season of "joyful expectation." The first two weeks of Advent focus on the coming of Christ at the end of time, while the second two weeks of Advent focus on the coming of the Christ Child on Christmas.

One of the themes of today's Scripture readings is that of perseverance, living one's life in harmony with God's plan. We do this by prayer, by vigilance, by living out our vocations faithfully day by day.

The man in the following story found out just how important perseverance is.

There was once a man named Scott who always wanted to be a cartoonist, but he didn't know how to go about becoming one. Then one day in 1986, as he was flipping through the television channels, he saw a program called *Funny Business*, a program about cartooning.

Scott immediately sent a letter to the cartoonist who had hosted the show, Jack Cassidy. He told Jack about his desire to become a cartoonist, but that he did not know how to go about it. Scott also sent Jack some samples of his work.

A few weeks later, Scott received a very encouraging, handwritten letter from Jack Cassidy. Jack answered all of Scott's questions, and told Scott that the samples he had sent were worthy of publication. But Jack told Scott that in the publishing business, rejection was common. Therefore, he told Scott to expect to be rejected at first but not to become discouraged.

Scott was very excited about Jack's kind words, so he got busy and sent his cartoons to two of America's top publications. Both publications immediately sent Scott rejection form letters. Discouraged, Scott put his art supplies in his closet and decided to forget cartooning.

In June of 1987, though, Scott received a second letter from Jack. The letter said that Jack had been going through some of his old files, and he once again came across Scott's original letter and cartoon samples. Jack told Scott that he hoped he had sent his samples to some publications and that he was on the road to making some money from them and having fun along the way.

Jack's letter particularly touched Scott because Jack had absolutely nothing to gain by writing it. And Scott had never even thanked Jack for the first letter he had received.

This letter of encouragement, therefore, profoundly touched Scott. So, he once again began sending out his cartoon samples to various newspapers and magazines.

Today, his cartoon feature—*Dilbert*—appears in several hundred newspapers and books. As Scott says, "Things are going pretty well in Dilbertville."

The story of Scott Adams, creator of the *Dilbert* comic strip, shows us two important principles: the power of encouragement, and the power of perseverance.

In the readings we have from 1 Thessalonians and St. Luke, we are encouraged to be ready for the coming of Christ by good living. This means that we live out our vocations faithfully each day. Most of us do not lead incredibly heroic lives. Rather, we do our best in our work and home lives as best we can.

Most people live their vocations by getting married, buying houses, raising children, going to work each day, and eventually retiring. Each and every day, they go through a routine composed of hundreds of activities— brushing their teeth, preparing food, washing dishes, changing diapers, putting gas in their cars, washing clothes, talking to coworkers and friends and family, and the like. Most of what we do is not what anyone would call "heroic."

The "heroic" part of our lives is not any specific activity that we do. Rather, it is that we live our vocations faithfully day after day, week after week, month after month, and year after year. That is called fidelity or perseverance. That is the mark of a solid person. That is what God is asking every one of us to do.

As for the virtue of encouragement, we are all called to assist one another on life's journeys. That is part of the triple love command of Jesus Christ, especially to love our neighbor. Just as Jack Cassidy encouraged Scott Adams in his cartoon career, we are expected to give each other encouragement.

As we enter into this season of Advent, let us take some time to reflect on how we model fidelity and perseverance to our own vocations, and how we encourage each other on the journey through life.

And that is the good news I have for you on this First Sunday of Advent.

Story source: Scott Adams, "A Kind Word," in Brian Cavanaugh's *Sower's Seeds of Encouragement: Fifth Planting,* New York: Paulist Press, 1998, #51, pp. 45-47.

Chapter 2

2nd Sunday of Advent – C
The Child and the Jewels

Scripture:

- Baruch 5: 1-9
- Psalm 126: 1-2ab, 2cd-3, 4-5, 6
- Philippians 1: 4-6, 8-11
- Luke 3: 1-6

Today we celebrate the Second Sunday of Advent. In the New Testament reading for today, we hear St. Paul telling the Philippians that God began good work in them, and that he will continue to complete it until the "day of Christ," that is, the Second Coming of Jesus.

Paul also gave the people some very practical advice on how they should live their lives as followers of Christ. He gave this advice with the full knowledge that life on this Earth is fleeting. Our sights should always be on the life in heaven. One particularly good admonition was to discern what is of value so that at the end of time, they would be filled with the fruit of righteousness. Today I examine the concept of "value" by starting with a story from Neil Kurshan's book, *Raising Your child to Be a Messiah.*

The was once a medical student who went to see a counselor about whether she should complete medical school or drop out to raise a family. The counselor told the young woman that she could do both with a little outside help. The student told the counselor that she had vowed to never entrust her children to a housekeeper. When the counselor asked her why she had made such a vow, the young woman explained that when she was a young child, her parents would vacation every summer and leave her with a nanny.

When the girl was eleven years old, the housekeeper suddenly quit her job shortly before the girl's parents were to leave for their annual summer vacation in Europe. The parents were very upset by the housekeeper's resignation, because it meant their vacation might have to be cancelled. However, a few days before their intended departure, they found a replacement who could look after the girl and the house while the parents were in Europe.

The mother began wrapping up all the family silverware and jewels, something she had never done before when taking a trip to Europe. When the little girl asked her mother why she was doing that, the mother explained that because she didn't really know the new housekeeper, she couldn't trust her with the family's valuables.

Needless to say, the little girl was crushed by this remark. After all, was she not a "family valuable?" Wasn't she worth more than silverware and jewels? She never forgot that day, and as she grew up, she promised herself that she would always raise her own children.

This is a wonderful story showing how at times our values can become distorted. But what is a "value" in St. Paul's view?

Dictionaries have many definitions of the word "value." Value, in St. Paul's terms, refers to something deeply held to have great intrinsic worth. In this view, a value is much more enduring than an opinion or an attitude, both of which can more easily be changed.

St. Paul is telling followers of Jesus to "discern what is of value" and act accordingly.

Contemplating our values is a great exercise, for it forces us to do some soul-searching and thinking. I maintain that as followers of Christ, the greatest value we can have is that of holiness. All other values are secondary. Unfortunately, we often forget this in our daily lives, as evidenced by how we talk and how we act. For example, when American parents talk about their adult children, they often say, "Well, I don't care what kind of work they have as long as they're...." What's the word they say? "Happy," of course.

But wouldn't it be more accurate, as Christian people, to end the sentence with "Holy?" Thus, a parent of an adult child would more appropriately say, "Well, I don't care what kind of work they have as long as they're holy." That, my friends, would more accurately reflect the deepest value we should have.

I maintain that all values we may have are secondary to that of holiness. Holiness is the core value for sainthood, and isn't that the ultimate goal of every Christian? Sainthood means going to heaven. All other goals we have in this life should be secondary. Holiness is the one goal that every human being with reason should attempt. Other goals are "iffy" at best.

For example, I get nervous when someone tells me their ultimate goal in life is to be a good spouse and parent. Though those are excellent goals, they should not be one's "ultimate" goal in life. A spouse could die, divorce could happen, a child might not be born, etc.

Others say their ultimate goal in life is to become a member of a particular profession. Well, that's a fine goal, but it shouldn't be an "ultimate" goal. You could be fired or you could suffer a stroke and not be able to practice your profession.

Others say their ultimate goal is something more abstract such as "I just want to be free." Well, maybe you'll end up in prison or confined to a wheelchair.

The only ultimate goal that you can achieve in this life regardless of any other factor is that of holiness. That is what St. Paul meant in his writings today.

What is your ultimate goal?

And that is the good news I have for you on this Second Sunday of Advent.

Story source: "Valuable," in William J. Bausch (Ed.), *A World of Stories for Preachers and Teachers,* 1998, #176, p. 309. (Based on the book *Raising Your Child to Be a Messiah,* by Neil Kurshan).

Chapter 3

3rd Sunday of Advent – C
Paderewski Meets Hoover

Scripture:

- Zephaniah 3: 14-18a
- Isaiah 12: 2-3, 4bcd, 5-6
- Philippians 4: 4-7
- Luke 3: 10-18

Today Catholic Christians celebrated the Third Sunday of Advent. The first thing we noticed today as we entered the church is that it must be a special occasion. The priest has a rose-colored vestment, the rose colored candle is list on our Advent wreath, the sanctuary is filled with a carpet of flowers, and there are hundreds of candles lit from the celebration of the Patron Saint of the Americas, Our Lady of Guadalupe. It's the Third Sunday of Advent.

On this day, we read an incredibly beautiful passage from St. Paul in his Letter to the Philippians. Among the various messages he gives, he tells the Christians that all should know them by their kindness.

Kindness is a virtue that shows itself in tenderness and concern for others, pleasantness, a mild disposition, and charity. The opposites of kindness are harshness and cruelty. Christians are called to show kindness for its own sake, not because they expect a reward for being kind. However, at times kindness can indeed result in rewards. That is exactly what happened to a man in the following story.

Several years ago, two young men were working their way through Stanford University. Because they were chronically penniless, they came up with a plan to make some money for themselves. They decided to invite a famous pianist, Paderewski, to do a recital. What they raised from the recital could then help them pay their room and board.

Mr. Paderewski's manager told the young men that they had to guarantee that the pianist would receive $2,000 from the event. That was a lot of money in those days, but the young men agreed and began to promote the concert. When the concert was finally held, they found that they had only grossed a mere $1,600.

After the concert, the two young men told the great artist the bad news, and they gave him the entire $1,600 along with a promissory note for $400. They told Mr. Paderewski that they would earn the remainder of the money as soon as they could and then send him the $400 they owed him. It seemed to them that this was the end of their college careers.

Mr. Paderewski, however, surprised them with unexpected kindness. He said, "No, boys, that won't do." Then, he tore up the promissory note and returned the $1,600 to them also. He then said, "Now I want you to take out of this $1,600 all of your expenses and keep ten percent of the balance for your school work. Let me have the remainder." Because of the kindness of Mr. Paderewski, the two young men were able to stay in college.

Some years passed, and World War I came and went. Mr. Paderewski, now Prime Minister of Poland, was struggling to feed thousands of his citizens who were starving. He knew that there was only one man in the whole world who could help him—Herbert Hoover, who was in charge of the United States Food & Relief Bureau at the time. Mr. Hoover was happy to help Premier Paderewski, and soon he sent thousands of tons of food to Poland.

After the starving people were fed, Premier Paderewski went to Paris to thank Mr. Hoover for his generosity. "That's all right, Mr. Paderewski," Mr. Hoover replied. "Besides, you don't remember it, but you helped me once when I was a student at college, and I was in trouble. Because of you, I was able to finish college."

Inspirational stories like this lead us to reflect on the theme at hand, in this case, the virtue of kindness.

A virtue is a character trait of a person that promotes well being. The opposite of a virtue is a vice. Virtues become strong when they are practiced over and over again. If we don't practice a particular virtue, it can fade and we may even develop vices to take their place. I like to think of virtues as the flowers in the garden of the soul. When they are tended and nourished with constant care, they flourish and are quite beautiful. When neglected, though, they wither and die and are crowded out with vices, the weeds of our spiritual gardens.

Fortunately for us, there are many opportunities to practice the virtue of kindness all around us. In fact, in our country there is even a movement that encourages people to practice what are called "random acts of kindness." The example that often comes to mind immediately is to pay the toll for a car coming behind you on a toll-road. I've done this myself from time to time, and I have had it done for me. It's a delightful feeling to help someone in a totally surprising way. Or, one may practice kindness by allowing someone with just a few groceries to go ahead in the checkout line at the grocery store. A simple smile can brighten up another's day and mean more than one can possibly imagine.

As we continue our life journeys this week, it would be a good idea to reflect on St. Paul's call for kindness in our lives. How do we show kindness to others? What kinds of rewards does kindness shower on others and us?

And that is the good news I have for you on this Third Sunday of Advent.

Story source: Anonymous, "Remember Those Who Help," in Brian Cavanaugh (Ed.), *Sower's Seeds of Encouragement: Fifth Planting,* New York: Paulist Press, 1998, #95, pp. 85-86.

Chapter 4

4ᵗʰ Sunday of Advent – C
The Austrian Physician

Scripture:

- Micah 5: 1-4a
- Psalm 80: 2ac & 3b, 15-16, 18-19
- Hebrews 10: 5-10
- Luke 1: 39-45

Today, we celebrate the Fourth Sunday of Advent, a Sunday when our thoughts are often more on Christmas than on Advent. Sometimes on this day, our mind is so filled with the coming holidays, family, and things we have to do, that we have a hard time focusing on the Scriptures.

Nevertheless, today we have a very important message in the Letter to the Hebrews. In this passage, we hear how Jesus told us that he came to do God's will. And, like Christ, we too are called to do God's will.

During the Advent and Christmas seasons, we hear all sorts of stories about Biblical figures doing God's will. Unfortunately, though, they learned God's will in ways not usually open to you and me. Mary, for example, learned God's will for her by a personal visit from an angel. Zechariah learned that he was to name his son John, by the same angel, Gabriel. Later, we'll learn that a special star in the sky guided wise men from the East, and we'll read how Joseph was told to flee to Egypt with his family to avoid having Jesus killed by Herod.

Now although God doesn't send us specific messages from angels and dreams and stars as he did in the Bible stories, he still talks to us in many ways. God helps us discern his will through books, stories, life experiences, school, television, family, friends, personal desires, daydreams, and many other ways.

Another way that some people come to understand God's will for them—often called "discerning God's will"—is by having life experiences so profound that they are touched to the very core of their being. Not everyone experiences such things, but in the following story, we learn how a young Austrian man did indeed experience something so dramatic that it led him to follow God in a very important way.

During World War II a young Austrian man was drafted into the German army, which at the time was invading Russia. One morning, on the outskirts of a village, his unit was ordered to stand in front of his commanding officer. After putting the men at ease, the commanding officer told the men that their unit had been ordered to shoot Jews. He then asked for volunteers to kill the Jews. When nobody volunteered, he began to call the men sniveling cowards and many other names that I can't repeat. Still, no soldier came forward.

Then the commanding officer tried again. This time, he said that the volunteers would not need to shoot the Jews immediately. First they could steal money and valuables from the Jews and use the Jewish women, and then they could kill them. After he said this, all of the men in the unit came forward except for three young men: a Jesuit seminarian, a gay actor from Berlin, and the young Austrian man.

At the end of the day, when the other soldiers returned to the barracks, the young Austrian man could not force himself to even be around the killers. So, because he was an excellent skier, he volunteered to go to the dangerous northern front, where he stayed until the end of the war. Because of this experience, he determined to become a physician and devote his life to healing instead of killing. And that is indeed what he did, and as a result, he was able to save lives.

When we hear stories such as this one, you may think them too far-fetched to apply to you, that they don't really have relevance in your life. But you would be wrong, for imbedded in this story and in the message of Jesus are some very important gems of practical wisdom for us. Here are just three of them.

First, as Christians, we are called to follow Christ. We are to imitate him. Thus, because Jesus was faithful in following God the Father's will in his life, we also are called to follow God's will.

Second, we can only be influenced by God's clues when we are open to them. This is often called living an "examined life." In other words, we need to be alert that every experience in our daily lives might be a clue to God's will for us. When we realize this, the world and our lives become incredibly fascinating. We begin to reflect the people in our lives, the situations in which we find ourselves, our struggles, our triumphs, our desires, our fantasies, our goals, our visions, and the like.

Third, we are to always be open to embracing God's clues in our lives and using them for good. For example, the young Austrian soldier could have easily have been so traumatized by his experience to become despaired or embittered. Have you ever met such people? I certainly have. I think of two such people with whom I went to high school. In high school they were filled with life and joy and fun. Today they are bitter people filled with anger and self-righteousness and intolerance. How incredibly sad this is.

When we are constantly ready to take our life experiences—bad and good—and use them to follow Christ in positive ways, we are truly on track, and we are opening ourselves to one of God's greatest gifts: serenity or peacefulness of the soul.

So as we continue our life journeys this week, let us ask God to help us be people of reflection, paying attention to the clues he is giving us each and every day on how we are to follow him.

And that is the good news I have for you on this Fourth Sunday of Advent.

Story source: "The Doctor's Vocation" in William J. Bausch (Ed.), *A World of Stories for Preachers and Teachers,* Mystic, CT: Twenty-Third Publications, 1998, #129, p. 277.

Chapter 5

Christmas - C
Candles in the Window

Scripture Mass During the Night:

- Isaiah 9: 1-6
- Psalm 96: 1-2a, 2b-3, 11-12, 13
- Titus 2: 11-14
- Luke 2: 1-14

On behalf of the staff, teachers, and all of the ministers of our parish, I wish you and those you love a very Merry Christmas! I pray that your Christmas hopes and dreams come true.

In the United States, there is no holiday that comes even close to the magic of Christmas. It is a season filled with fantastic stories, beautiful lights, special music, and tempting foods. A week ago, for example, I went to a little church called Our Lady of the Snows in Elizabethtown, N.C. There I conducted an Advent Reconciliation Service for the people. And as I traveled the dark, rural North Carolina roads, I listened to Christmas carols and enjoyed seeing houses lit up for Christmas.

One of the most common decorations were candles in the windows, not real candles, but electric ones. I reflected that though these candles are pretty in and of themselves, I wondered how many of the people who had these candles knew about the origins of the custom.

According to many historians, the Irish immigrants brought the custom of having candles in the windows at Christmastime to the United States. There was a time when the English rulers outlawed Catholic Christianity in Ireland. The Catholic people had no churches in which to worship, and Masses were illegal. Catholic priests, who at times were subject to instant execution if found, had to hide in the forests and caves and other places, and would celebrate Mass in the farms and homes of Catholics in the dark of night.

It was a deep wish of every Irish Catholic family that at least once in their lifetime, a priest would come to their home at Christmas to celebrate the Mass. For this wish, they prayed all through the night of Christmas Eve and left their doors unlocked. They would put burning candles in the windows so that any priest who happened to be in the neighborhood would know that this was a house in which he would be welcomed. A passing priest would be guided by the candles in the windows, and could enter the house silently through the unlocked door. The lucky family would receive him with tears of joy and prayers of gratitude, honored that their home would become a church for Christmas Mass.

At first, the English authorities wondered why the Irish Catholics were putting candles in their windows on Christmas Eve. Of course, the people could not tell the truth or the priests' lives would be endangered. Therefore, they told the English, "We burn the candles in the windows and keep our doors unlocked so that Mary and Joseph, while looking for a place to stay, will find their way to our home and be welcomed with open doors and open hearts." The English authorities, finding this Irish Catholic "superstition" harmless, did not bother to suppress the custom. As a result, candles in the windows remained an Irish custom through the ages even though many people forgot exactly why they did it.

In the early nineteenth century, the Irish immigrants brought the custom of candles in the window to the United States. Soon, it spread throughout the whole country.

Today we continue this practice, not to welcome priests on Christmas Eve, but rather to show that we live in homes that are places of light, of hope, of dreams, and of joy. The candles in the window tell the world that dwelling in this home are believers in Jesus Christ, the Messiah promised many centuries ago by God to the Hebrew people.

You may be interested to know that candles in the window are not only a symbol of Christmas. They are also a symbol of solidarity with others' hopes and dreams. I myself saw such candles glowing in the windows of people who wanted to see the downfall of Communism in their country. It was the week of the "Velvet Revolution" in Czechoslovakia, and I was at Charles University giving some lectures. Each day, thousands and thousands of people would pour into Wenceslaus Square to hear speeches and to chant and sing for freedom. As I was in the Square, I would look up at windows in the buildings surrounding us, and sure enough, there would be many windows in which candles were glowing. Candles would also burn in little homemade shrines on sidewalks throughout Prague.

From that experience, I came to appreciate the power of light and dreams and hopes. No matter how horrible the situation is around us, and no matter how hard forces of evil try to destroy, they can never vanquish dreams and hopes. That is, of course, the miracle of Christmas. The Light of the World came to us disguised as a poor baby. And before leaving the world, he commanded us to keep the light glowing by being "lights to the world." And to this day, the light still shines even during the darkest of nights.

So the next time you see a candle glowing in the window, it would be good to think of how much it symbolizes our faith. How bright is your light?

I pray that the light of Christmas always shine in your hearts and homes.

And that is the good news I have for you on this Christmas Day.

Story source: "The Birth of the Lord," in Gerard Fuller (Ed.), *Stories for All Seasons*, Mystic, CT: Twenty-Third Publications, 1996, p. 9.

Chapter 6

Holy Family – C
Build Me a Son

Scripture:

- Sirach 3: 2-6, 12-14
- Psalm 128: 1-2, 3, 4-5
- Colossians 3: 12-21
- Luke 2: 41-52

Today the Church celebrates the Feast of the Holy Family of Jesus, Mary, and Joseph.

In today's Gospel reading, we hear how this family went to Jerusalem, as was their custom, to celebrate Passover. Jesus was twelve years old at the time. After the celebrations were over, Jesus stayed behind to listen to and talk with the elders in the temple. After a day's journey, Mary and Joseph discovered that Jesus was not in the caravan. Like any parents who lose a child, they must have been frantic. After returning to Jerusalem, they found him in the temple. The Scripture then says that Jesus went back with them to Nazareth and was obedient to them. Further, he "advanced in wisdom and age and favor before God and man" (Luke 2: 52).

There is very little in the Scriptures about Jesus before his public ministry began when he was thirty years old. However, we can imagine that he must have learned something about carpentry from Joseph, studied the Hebrew Scriptures, and celebrated Jewish holidays.

But though we don't know specifics about Jesus' childhood and adolescence, are not the wishes of parents basically the same throughout the ages? Don't parents wish the very best for their children? I think so. In fact, I recently came across a prayer created by one of the pre-eminent military men of World War II, General Douglas MacArthur. In his "A Prayer for My Son," I think he captures what every parent might hope for. And though it discusses a son, everything contained in the prayer pertains perfectly to a daughter.

A Prayer for My Son
by
Gen. Douglas MacArthur

Build me a son, O Lord,
  who will be strong enough to know when he is weak,
  brave enough to face himself when he is afraid;
  one who will be proud and unbending in honest defeat,
  and humble and gentle in victory.
Build me a son,
  whose wishes will not take the place of deeds;

a son who will know You and that to know himself is
the foundation stone of knowledge.
Lead him, I pray, not in the path of ease and comfort,
but under the stress and spur of difficulties and
challenges.
Let him learn to stand in the storm;
let him learn compassion for those who fall.
Build me a son,
whose heart is clear, whose goals will be high;
a son who will master himself before he seeks to master
others;
who will reach into the future, yet never forget the past.
And after all these things are his, add, I pray,
enough of a sense of humor
so that he may always be serious
yet never take himself too seriously.
Give him humility, so that he may always remember
the simplicity of true greatness,
the open mind of true wisdom,
and the meekness of true strength.
Then, I, his father will dare to whisper,
'I have not lived in vain.'"

What a beautiful prayer this is. Wouldn't any parent want this for their daughter or son? Wouldn't any parent be proud to have raised a child to become the person wished for in the prayer?

And when we look at Jesus' life, didn't he live up to the ideals set forth in the prayer?

Like the Holy Family, today's families also strive to create the "ideal" son or daughter. Though they are less than perfect, they do the best they can with what they have. And because raising children is such an enormous task, parents need all the graces they can get to help them in their vocation.

So as we continue our life journeys this week, let's ask God to shower his special graces on all families to help them be cradles of love and strength.

And that is the good news I have for you on this Feast of the Holy Family.

Story source: Gen. Douglas MacArthur, "A Prayer for My Son," found on several WWW sites.

Chapter 7

Epiphany of the Lord – C
Jackie Robinson

Scripture:

- Isaiah 60: 1-6
- Psalm 72: 1-2, 7-8, 10-11, 12-13
- Ephesians 3: 2-3a, 5-6
- Matthew 2: 1-12

Today we celebrate the Feast of the Epiphany, also known as "Little Christmas" or the Feast of the Three Kings. This ancient feast has been celebrated in the Catholic Church even longer than Christmas Day itself. In the Western branches of the Catholic Church to which we belong, the feast celebrates the showing of Jesus to the wise men from the East who brought gifts to Jesus.

As a child, many of us were taught the significance of the gifts the wise men brought to Jesus. The gold symbolized his kingship; the frankincense symbolized his divinity; and the sweet-smelling myrrh symbolized his eventual crucifixion.

But probably the most important thing about the Feast of the Epiphany is that Jesus came for all people, not just the Hebrews. For those of us living two thousand years after Jesus walked the earth, we take this for granted. But for the early Church, this was very big news indeed.

Although including others into a group has always been difficult for human beings, we are to "welcome the stranger" among us. We are to proclaim the good news of Jesus Christ to all people. We are to welcome all to worship at the banquet table of the Lord. We are to people of "inclusion," not "exclusion."

In the following story, we hear how important the principle of inclusion was to a very famous baseball player by the name of Jackie Robinson.

In 1947, Jackie Robinson became the first black player in Major League Baseball. In those days, prejudice and discrimination against African-Americans were rampant in American society. The President and General Manager of the Brooklyn Dodgers team, Branch Rickey, took a chance on giving Jackie Robinson a job. He told Jackie, "It will be very tough on you. You will take a lot of abuse, be ridiculed, and will receive more verbal punishment that you ever thought possible. However, I am willing to back you up if you have the determination to make it work."

Very quickly, Jackie found that what Rickey had predicted came true. The crowd was often verbally abusive towards Jackie, and players were often not only verbally abusive, but they would deliberately run over him or crash into him while running the bases. Even his own teammates ridiculed him.

Around the middle of his first season with the Brooklyn Dodgers, Jackie was having a particularly bad day. He had fumbled several ground balls, overthrown first base, and batted poorly. The crowd was especially nasty that day.

Then, something amazing happened. In front of this hostile crowd, Pee Wee Reese, the team captain, walked over to Jackie from his shortstop position and gave Jackie Robinson a friendly hug.

Jackie later reflected, "That simple gesture saved my career. Pee Wee made me feel as if I belonged."

This story of inclusion captures in a very concrete way the main message of the Epiphany. Just as Jackie was welcomed as a team member even though he was at first considered an outsider, followers of Jesus Christ are to welcome all who come to worship the Lord.

When we look back on the two thousand years of Catholic Christianity, however, we see that many times we have failed to be inclusive. Orthodox and Protestant Christians, I should add, are not immune to failure in inclusion either. Here are just a few of the many examples in which Catholic Christians have failed to be inclusive within their own Church.

In our own country, we have had a history of treating people differently because of their skin color. In many dioceses of the United States, there were different churches for African-Americans and white Americans.

Other Catholic Christians have developed exclusionary attitudes based on feelings of moral superiority. These are people who sit in judgment of others, and they decide to discriminate against people who do not measure up to their own belief system. There are even people who call themselves the "Real Catholics" and anyone who does not share their passions they consider to be "Catholics in Name Only."

Some Catholics discriminate against people because they don't like the way they dress. They treat people with tattoos or nose rings or raggedy jeans as second-class Catholics. They often show their displeasure with glaring looks or refusing to offer a friendly smile or greeting.

Other Catholics may show contempt for people in their parish who come from another land or who speak a different language. Instead of following Christ's command to welcome the stranger, they treat such newcomers to their parish community with downright contempt or simply ignore them.

Withholding love from others flies in the face of Christ's triple love command. When we withhold love, we fail to see Christ in fellow human beings. This is wrong.

As we continue our life journey this week, it would be a good idea to examine our own consciences to see if we have any weeds of exclusion in our spiritual gardens, weeds that we need to dig up and discard as soon as possible.

And that is the good news I have for you on this Feast of the Epiphany.

Story source: Anonymous, "A Simple Gesture," in Brian Cavanaugh (Ed.), *Fresh Packet of Sower's Seeds: 3rd Planting,* New York: Paulist Press, 1994, #59, pp. 55-56.

Chapter 8

Baptism of the Lord - C
Jean Donovan

Scripture:

- Isaiah 42: 1-4, 6-7
- Psalm 29: 1a & 2, 3ac-4, 3b & 9b-10
- Acts 10: 34-38
- Luke 3: 15-16, 21-22

Today the Church celebrates the Feast of the Baptism of Jesus by his cousin, John the Baptist. Though he had no need of baptism because he had no sin on his soul, Jesus' baptism served three purposes. First, it showed his solidarity with humanity. Second, it marked his public ministry. And third, it provided a first glimpse of the Trinity by having the Holy Spirit appear as a dove, with God the Father telling the people in the event that Jesus was his Son.

The Catholic Church in the United States uses this Feast to begin a weeklong celebration called the National Vocation Awareness Week. This is truly fitting, for our vocations come from our baptism. Though all of us have vocations or callings, the Church is focusing its attention this week on church vocations. These include calls to the Religious Life (which includes Religious Sisters, Brothers, and priests who are members of religious orders), calls to lay ecclesial ministries such as lay missionaries and lectors, Extraordinary Ministers of the Eucharist, catechists, directors of religious education, etc., and calls to the ordained priesthood.

On this occasion, we look into the life of a young woman whom God led into a Church vocation as a lay missionary. The woman's name was Jean Donovan.

Jean was raised in an upper middle-class home in Connecticut. After receiving her bachelor's degree from a college in Virginia, she spent a year as an exchange student in Ireland. There she had regular contact with a priest who had been a missionary in Peru.

When she returned to the United States, Jean earned a Master's degree in Business Administration from Case Western Reserve University in Cleveland, and soon was working as a management consultant for the Cleveland branch of the nationwide accounting firm of Arthur Andersen.

Jean became engaged to a young physician, and began doing volunteer work for the Diocese of Cleveland's Youth Ministry with the poor. While working with the poor, Jean felt a strong call to become a lay missionary. This was not an easy decision, and sometimes she wondered why God would not let her be content as a quiet homemaker. However, God called, and Jean followed.

She went to Maryknoll, NY, where she completed a course for lay missionaries, and in July 1977 went to El Salvador to join the Diocese of Cleveland's mission there. In La Libertad, El Salvador, Jean worked with an Ohio Ursuline nun, Sr. Dorothy Kazel. At this time, El Salvador was experiencing a civil war in which 75,000 people would eventually be killed. The country was rocked with violence between right-wing government forces and the left-wing guerilla organizations that formed to combat the abuses of the government. Jean and Sr. Dorothy provided shelter, food, and health care. They transported victims of the conflict, and they buried the dead. Jean, who played guitar at Masses, quickly became known for her incredible sense of humor. It was as though she had been born to make people laugh with her wisecracks and jokes. People began calling her "St. Jean the Playful."

Like other missionaries in El Salvador, Jean was a devotee of the great Archbishop of San Salvador, Oscar Romero. After Oscar Romero was killed at the Cathedral, in March of 1980, Sister Dorothy and Jean Donovan kept watch all night at his coffin on the night of his wake.

Naturally, Jean's family and friends were very frightened for her safety, and they urged Jean to come back to the United States. That was not in Jean's plans.

On December 2, 1980, Jean gave an interview with a journalist named Pat. She told Pat that she had considered leaving El Salvador many times, but she couldn't leave as the people were deep in her heart. As part of the interview, when Pat asked Jean why she was staying in the midst of such danger instead of returning to Cleveland and safety, Jean answered:

> "My work is here. The government's death squads and the guerillas kill the villagers. They leave the children orphans. How can I turn my back on them? They need food and shelter. They need someone to hold them at night when they cry."

Later that day, December 2, 1980, Jean and Sr. Dorothy drove to the San Salvador airport to pick up their two Maryknoll friends, Sr. Maura Clarke and Sr. Ita Ford, who were returning from a Maryknoll conference in Managua, Nicaragua. What the women didn't know, was that government agents had them under surveillance.

As the four women drove from the airport, they were stopped by five members of the Salvadorian National Guard and taken to an isolated place. There they were beaten, raped, and killed.

A film called *Roses in December* highlights the life and death of Jean Donovan.

As we continue our life journeys this week, it would be good to ask ourselves where our baptism call will lead us. Are we up to answering God's call?

And that is the good news I have for you on this Feast of the Baptism of Jesus.

Story sources:

- Ana Carrigan and Bernard Stone, *Roses in December* (Documentary), 1982.
- Judith Noone, *The Same Fate As the Poor*, Maryknoll, NY: Orbis Books, 1984, 1995.

Part Two

LENT &
EASTER SEASONS

Chapter 9

1st Sunday of Lent - C
The Coffee Cake Temptation

Scripture:

- Deuteronomy 26: 4-10
- Psalm 91: 1-2, 10-11, 12-13, 14-15
- Romans 10: 8-13
- Luke 4: 1-13

On this First Sunday of Lent, we once again hear the wonderful story of Jesus being tempted by the devil in the desert. Jesus, of course, rejects all of the temptations for food, power, glory, and worldly riches.

We, too, are called to reject the temptations we find may find in our lives. As a matter of fact, every time we come to celebrate the Eucharist, we sing or say the Lord's Prayer, which says, in part, "Lead us not into temptation."

Many times, though, we say the words without really meaning them. That can happen when we do things so many times; they lose their effect on us. Or, we only mean this half-heartedly; we like to "flirt" with temptation. That is what happened to the man in the following story whom I'll call Ethan.

Ethan was overweight and unhappy about it. Being a good Catholic man, Ethan decided to strengthen his spiritual life for Lent by showing that "the spirit is greater than the flesh." Specifically, he decided to lose a lot of weight. He was so excited about his plan that he told everyone in his office that he was going on a low-calorie diet. Everyone in the office was very supportive of Ethan and his quest to lose weight.

Ethan even took steps to reduce tempting foods. In fact, he even changed his usual driving route from home to work to avoid going past his favorite bakery.

One morning, however, Ethan showed up at the office carrying a large, sugarcoated, calorie-loaded cake. His office mates were very disappointed in him.

Ethan, though, explained how this was a very special cake, one that God Himself wanted him to have. Ethan explained that out of pure habit, he had accidently turned down the old street where his favorite bakery was located. He thought to himself, "This must not have been an accident. Maybe God wanted me to go past the bakery to show me how strong I am." As he slowly went by the bakery, he saw that it had the most delicious cake he ever saw in the window. So, Ethan talked to God and said, "God, I will drive around the block. If you want me to have that cake, then show me a sign. Make there be an empty parking space directly in front of the bakery." And, Ethan explained to his colleagues, "On the ninth time around the block, there was an empty parking space directly in front of the bakery just for me!"

What makes this story so funny is that at times we have acted just like Ethan. We have "tempted temptation" so to speak. But what are temptations and how can we maturely deal with them?

Temptations are enticements calling us to something. Though temptations can be to engage in something positive, such as being tempted to help those in need, when Jesus was talking about temptations he was referring to the negative kind.

It's important to remember that temptations, in themselves, are neither good nor bad; they just are. What is bad, though, is when we allow them to lead us to behave in ways not appropriate for a follower of Jesus Christ.

As we get older, we realize that it is better to avoid people, places, and situations that tempt us. Often, this is simply a matter of common sense and planning.

Take, for example, problematic people. There may be those who make us very angry or depressed. Whenever we are around them, we leave in a bad mood. This, in turn, affects our work, our relationships with loved ones, and our mental health. The best thing to do is to avoid these people if we possibly can. If we cannot avoid them, such as colleagues or in-laws, we can minimize our contacts with them. We can wear an invisible shield and vow not to get sucked up in their negativity.

Avoiding people who like to gossip or who coax us into doing bad things is also something we could do.

Sometimes it is not people who are the problem as much as situations. When we know certain situations are dangerous for us, we are obliged to avoid them whenever possible. That is why Alcoholics Anonymous does not hold meetings in bars and Overeaters' Anonymous doesn't hold meetings in bakeries. If people have problems with spending, it would be a good idea to avoid cruising malls with a credit card, just as it would be a good idea not to go onto chat rooms on the Internet if they seem to be the occasion of sin.

Finally, certain things in our lives could be problematic. We can't seem to use them in moderation. These "things" could be such obvious items as alcohol or food, or they could be more nebulous things such as the desire for power or prestige. Desiring such things in itself is not a problem. It is when we misuse items or engage in undesirable behaviors to achieve them that is the problem.

During Lent, Catholic Christians try to strengthen their spiritual lives. Often they follow the three pillars of Lent: fasting, almsgiving, and prayer. Sometimes they give up something pleasurable to show that the spirit is stronger than the flesh, or they add something positive in their lives for the same reason.

As we continue our life journeys this week, it would be a good idea to ask ourselves not only how to avoid temptation but also how we tend to "flirt" with temptation.

And that is the good news I have for you on this First Sunday of Lent.

Story source: "Temptation," in William J. Bausch, (Ed.), *A World of Stories for Preachers and Teachers*, Mystic, CT: Twenty-Third Publications, 1998, #338, p. 390.

Chapter 10

2nd Sunday of Lent – C
The Graduation Gift

Scripture:

- Genesis 15: 5-12, 17-18
- Psalm 27: 1, 7-8, 9abc, 13-14
- Philippians 3: 17 – 4: 1
- Luke 9: 28b-36

As we come together to celebrate the Eucharist today, we once again encounter the fascinating story of the Transfiguration.

In this story, we see Jesus taking three of his disciples—Peter, James, and John—up on a mountain to pray. Suddenly, while Jesus was praying, his face changed in appearance, and his clothes became dazzling white. And, to the amazement of the disciples, Moses and Elijah appeared on the scene and were talking with Jesus. The disciples wanted to build three tents to honor Jesus, Elijah, and Moses to show their reverence for the three. But while the disciples were presenting their plan, suddenly a shadow fell over them, and God said, "This is my chosen Son; listen to him" (Luke 9: 35). Then, Moses and Elijah disappeared, leaving only Jesus for the disciples to gaze at.

This wonderful story has much to teach us. The most important thing, I think, is that it is a strong reminder to us to keep our eyes on Jesus. Just as the Old Testament prophecy will pass away, symbolized by the prophet Elijah, and just as the Old Testament law will pass away, symbolized by the lawgiver Moses, the things of this world will also pass away. Therefore, people, places, and things of this world should not dazzle us.

Unfortunately, though, sometimes we do fall so deeply in love with things of this world that we make fools of ourselves. That is what happened to the young man in the following story called "The Graduation Gift."

There was once a young man named Joe who was about to graduate from high school. He came from a very wealthy family that lived in a very affluent neighborhood. In this neighborhood, it was the custom of parents to give their sons and daughters a new car as a graduation present when they graduated from high school.

Months before Joe's graduation, he and his father visited many car dealerships looking at cars until they found the perfect one. Joe was convinced that at his graduation party, his dad would joyfully hand him the keys to a new car.

On the eve of Joe's graduation, his family threw him a big party. When the gifts were being opened, Joe was devastated when his father handed him a gift-wrapped Bible! Joe was so angry that he threw the Bible across the room and stormed out of the house, vowing never to return again. And Joe kept his word; he stopped all communications with his father and never saw his father again. Many years passed, and one day

Joe received word that his father had died. The death brought Joe back to his father's house.

A couple of days after the funeral, as Joe went through his father's possessions that he was to inherit, he came across the Bible that his dad had given him for a graduation gift. He brushed away the dust and opened it. To his amazement, he found a cashier's check, dated the day of his graduation, for the exact amount of the car that he and his dad had chosen together.

What an incredibly sad story this is. In the case of Joe, his greed had consumed him and, as a result, he became a bitter man. Imagine how his father, who had so wanted to surprise and please his son, must have suffered because of the estrangement!

As Christians, we too are called to keep our eyes on Jesus and not get distracted by other things. As people living in 21st-century America, we are surrounded by an incredible array of goods and services and people to tempt us. Some people do indeed fall in love with what they are surrounded with. They may fall in love with houses, cars, fancy clothes, vacations, or an infinite variety of "stuff." They find they can't go a week without buying more and more "things," things they want but don't need. They begin to lose the ability to distinguish between "needs" and "wants."

Others fall in love with power and prestige. They want to get into positions where they can control other people or have people give them special treatment and praise.

Some fall in love with political parties. Some become so in love that they can't distinguish their Christian creed from that of their political party. That can be dangerous, for such blind allegiance prevents people from seeing the flaws in their political parties.

Because Catholic Christians have such a rich history of ritualistic worship, they have to be especially careful not to fall in love with rituals in and of themselves. They need to remember that rituals are designed to help us worship God in an organized and unified way. Rituals should never been seen as idols, something to be worshipped.

Sometimes people worship themselves. They see themselves as morally superior to other people. They judge others harshly and come to the conclusion that, indeed, they are truly better than others. Thus, they go through life quick to condemn anyone who does not think and act as they do. Tragically, they fail to remember that Christ lives in every human being and are, therefore, disrespectful to the Jesus Christ who lives in others.

People may also make idols out of preachers on television or radio, blindly following whatever such personalities preach. When we fall in love with religious figures, we are in danger of taking the evil of what they preach along with the good; all their preaching becomes equal in our eyes.

As we continue our life journeys this week, let's take some time to examine our own lives. What kinds of idols do we have? How do we take our eyes off Jesus?

And that is the good news I have for you on this Second Sunday of Lent.

Story source: Anonymous, "The Graduation Gift," in Brian Cavanaugh (Ed.), *Sower's Seeds That Nurture Family Values; Sixth Planting,* New York: Paulist Press, 2000, #75, pp. 81-82.

Chapter 11

3rd Sunday of Lent – C
Butterfly over the Heart

Scripture:

- Exodus 3: 1-8a, 13-15
- Psalm 103: 1-2, 3-4, 6-7, 8 & 11
- 1 Corinthians 10: 1-6, 10-12
- Luke 13: 1-9

In today's Gospel reading for the Third Sunday of Lent, Jesus tells his disciples the parable of the poor fig tree that for three years in a row did not produce figs. In other words, it did not live up to what it was created to do. The owner of the tree was ready to have it cut down, but the gardener pleaded with the owner to give the tree another chance. The tree's owner agreed.

In this parable, Jesus is the gardener, always ready to help us achieve our potential. He is the gardener of our souls, always ready to bring us special help to grow and flourish.

Jesus often works through you and me to reach others, to help them have another chance in their lives. That is exactly what happened to the doctor in the following story. God worked through him to help a little boy get a second chance in life.

One summer, Dr. Tim Jordan volunteered as a summer camp counselor. At camp, he met a ten-year old boy named David.

David had an alcoholic father who often flew into rages and was abusive towards his son. When Dr. Tim met David, he noticed that David always walked around with slumped shoulders and did not look others in the eye. He was emotionally distant from others, even from the other kids. He got into a fight at camp on his very first day.

On the third day of camp, during a group processing session, David experienced a breakthrough. David opened up and told the group members about his dad and the abuse he experienced regularly. He talked about his fear and anger and sadness and feelings of powerless and isolation. He sobbed as he spoke and let go of some of the emotional pain that he had been carrying around for all his young years.

Now David began to open up and began to trust others. For the first time in years, he began to invite adults and other kids into his life.

On the day before camp was to end, though, David got into a fight. He had not shown such behavior since the day he had first arrived at camp. Counselors know that this is common behavior for children who fear going back to an abusive home.

Dr. Tim, therefore, took David for a walk and began to talk to him. Dr. Tim told David how proud he was of him for all the work he had done at camp and how he had been able to open up. He congratulated him on how David had begun to trust others and how much he had changed. David listened carefully but did not say anything.

Suddenly, a beautiful butterfly landed in their path. Dr. Tim told David about a Native American Indian belief that when a butterfly crosses one's path, a great transformation would take place.

David looked up with the same sad eyes that he had when he had first arrived at camp and said, "But what if the butterfly is for you, and not for me?"

Dr. Tim didn't know what to say. But suddenly, the butterfly flew around and landed on David's shirt, right above his heart. There was no need for words. Total joy and hope filled David's eyes. The words and kindness of Dr. Tim, and the butterfly, were the ingredients that allowed David to undergo a transformation.

Like the gardener who pleaded with the owner of the fig tree to give the tree another chance, Dr. Tim took David under his wing to help him have another chance at life. God used Dr. Tim as his instrument to touch the mind and heart of a child and create a transformation.

Jesus is like the gardener in the story of the fig tree. No matter how many times we fail to live up to our potential, Jesus puts in a good word for us. He continually argues for a second chance for us. He continually is convinced that he has the necessary ingredients to help us undergo a transformation in our lives. This is, of course, wonderful news, especially during the season of Lent when we are called to transform ourselves.

Just as the gardener gave the fig tree special attention and fertilizer to help it begin producing figs as it was created to do, Jesus gives us special attention and help. These gifts of help include family and friends to encourage us on our life journey, the values taught to us as children, the blessings of our jobs, education, health, ambition, and opportunities we get from the country we live in. And as Catholic Christians, we are specially blessed with the graces that flow from the sacraments we celebrate. In other words, God showers us with an incredible array of special graces to help us transform ourselves each and every day to become the people we were created to be.

As we continue our life journeys this week, it would be good to take some time to reflect on the many ways that God is showering us with graces. It would be good to not only list such sources of help he gives us, but to question how we thank him for them. And finally, it would be good to ask ourselves how we, ourselves, are at times his instruments through which he works to help others in their growth and transformation.

And that is the good news I have for you on this Third Sunday of Lent.

Story source: Dr. Tim Jordan, "The Miracle of Love," in Jack Canfield & Mark Victor Hansen (Eds.), *A 5th portion of chicken soup for the soul,* Deerfield, FL: Health Communications, Inc., 1998, pp. 305-308.

Chapter 12

4th Sunday of Lent – C
Forgiveness in a Cookie Bag

Scripture:

- Joshua 5: 9a, 10-12
- Psalm 34: 2-3, 4-5, 6-7
- 2 Corinthians 5: 17-21
- Luke 15: 1-3, 11-32

In today's Gospel reading for the Fourth Sunday of Lent, Jesus tells his disciples the story commonly known as the "Parable of the Prodigal Son." It is a story not only of a young man who turned his life around after he had "hit bottom," but it is also a beautiful story of forgiveness.

As Christians, we are called to forgive our enemies or those who hurt us. In fact, at each Mass, we ask God to forgive us in the same way we forgive those who hurt us.

Some people have a very difficult time with the concept of forgiveness. They want revenge. Others, though, have a much easier time following Jesus Christ, for they are ready to forgive just as quickly as the father in the story of the Prodigal Son. Such a person was the lady in the following story told by Jerry Harpt.

In 1954, Jerry was a twelve-year old boy living in Marinette, Wisconsin.

One Saturday afternoon, he and his friend were throwing rocks onto the roof of an old woman's house from a secluded spot in her backyard. The woman was one of Jerry's customers on his paper route. The object of their play was to see how the rocks would roll down the roof and shoot out into the yard like meteorites from the sky.

All was going well until Jerry found a very smooth rock to throw. It was too smooth, though, so when he threw it, it slipped from his hand and went straight into a window on the old lady's porch, breaking it. At the sound of the glass shattering, Jerry and his friend quickly ran out of the yard so they wouldn't get caught.

That night, Jerry was scared, because he was not sure that the old lady had not seen him. However, after a few days, when he was sure he had not been discovered, he began to be filled with guilt. Each day when he delivered her paper, the old lady greeted him warmly, but he was too filled with guilt to look her in the eye.

So, Jerry decided to save the money he made delivering papers and pay her for the broken window. After three weeks, he had been able to put seven dollars together; that is what he estimated a new window would cost. Jerry put the money into an envelope with a note explaining that he was sorry he broke the window and hoped that the seven dollars would cover the cost for repairing it. He did not sign the letter.

Jerry waited until it was dark, sneaked up to the old lady's house, and put the envelope through the letter slot in her door. He felt his guilt melt away, and he was looking forward to being able to look the lady straight into her eyes once again.

The next day, the old lady was at the door when he was delivering his papers, and he gladly returned her greeting and smile. After thanking him for the paper as she always did, she said, "Here, Jerry, I have something for you." She then handed him a bag of cookies. After thanking her for the cookies, Jerry began to eat them as he continued on his paper route.

After eating several cookies, he felt an envelope and pulled it out of the bag. When he opened the envelope, he was shocked. Inside, he found the seven dollars he had left and a short note that read, "I'm proud of you!"

This story, like that of the parable of the Prodigal Son, contains many lessons.

First, in both of the stories, there is a person who did wrong. In the prodigal son story, the wrong was deliberate. The young man ran away and squandered his inheritance. In the cookie story, breaking the window was not really wrong, it was a mistake. But he made a bigger mistake by fleeing the scene and not owning up to what he had done.

Second, in both of the stories, the guilty person is filled with remorse. The prodigal son is filled with regret because he has been forced to live in abject poverty, and Jerry is filled with guilt. In both instances, the guilty persons are very uncomfortable.

Third, in both stories the guilty parties want to make amends. They want to have the negative feelings stop. The prodigal son wants to once again be able to be clean and have plenty to eat, and Jerry wants to be free from the guilt that is consuming him. Therefore, they both decide to make amends.

Fourth, and very importantly, the persons who have been harmed are more than ready to forgive. In the case of the prodigal son, the father is overwhelmed with joy at his son's return. Although the son tries to say he's sorry, the father hardly even hears the words because he is too busy planning a giant celebration. In the case of the old woman, she knew all along that it was Jerry who broke her window. She treated him with kindness every day, even before he slipped her the envelope. And she would have continued to do that even if Jerry had never sent the money.

God is like the father in the prodigal son story, and God is like the old woman in the cookie story. God knows our faults and loves us anyway. There is nothing we can ever do to destroy his love for us, for we are his children. Although he may be disappointed in how we behave at times, he will never stop loving us.

As we continue our life journeys this week, it would be good to ask ourselves how we forgive others. Are we like the father in the prodigal son story? Are we like the old lady with the cookies? Or do we refuse to reflect God's love and mercy?

And that is the good news I have for you on this Fourth Sunday of Lent.

Story source: Jerry Harpt, "True Forgiveness," in Jack Canfield & Mark Victor Hansen (Eds.), *A 5ᵗʰ Portion of Chicken Soup for the Soul*, Deerfield, FL: Health Communications, Inc., 1998, pp. 361-362.

Chapter 13

5th Sunday of Lent – C
Forgiveness in the Troubles

Scripture:

- Isaiah 43: 16-21
- Psalm 126: 1-2ab, 2cd-3, 4-5, 6
- Philippians 3: 8-14
- John 8: 1-11

The closer we get to Easter, the more the Scripture passages talk about forgiveness and reconciliation. Last week, for example, we heard the beautiful story of the Prodigal Son and how a father forgave his son so readily when he returned.

Today, on this Fifth Sunday of Lent, we hear another beautiful story of forgiveness. In this story, we see a woman who was caught in adultery. Many people were ready to stone her to death, but first they had to encounter Jesus. He then began to write something in the sand and said, "Let the one among you who is without sin be the first to throw a stone at her" (John 8: 7). One by one they left the scene. All that were left were Jesus and the woman. He readily forgave her and told her to sin no more.

Forgiveness is an incredibly important message for Jesus, for he tells us about it in many of his teachings. Putting it into practice, though, is often difficult, as we know. But also difficult is the other big message we hear in today's story: do not judge others.

In the following story, we see two people who judged each other harshly. But they did not stop there. On the contrary, they got to know each other's worldviews and, as a result, began to understand each other and their worlds. Furthermore, they began to take their message of forgiveness and non-judgment of others to the whole world.

Jo Berry was a young woman from Great Britain. Her father was a member of the British Parliament. In 1984, a bomb thrown by a member of the Irish Republican Army (IRA) killed Jo's father.

From the very beginning, Jo knew that she did not want to become a bitter person as a result of the bombing. She knew that the only way to do that was to somehow bring something positive out of this tragic experience.

To start this journey, in November of 2000 Jo went to meet Patrick Magee, the bomber who killed her father. Patrick had been released from prison in what has become known as the Good Friday Agreement, an agreement to resolve many differences between the British and Irish governments.

Jo was very scared when she went to meet Patrick. She had no idea what he was like, and she had no idea how the meeting would go. However, she and Patrick got along very well. In fact, their meeting lasted three hours. They did not simply gloss over events. Rather, they each shared their worldviews, the very basic factors that made them who they were. Patrick described what it was like to be a minority Catholic person who had experienced continual discrimination and frustration. Jo described what it was like to have family and friends, who had done nothing wrong, become victims of violence.

The meetings between Jo and Patrick continued, and they became good friends. In fact, both of their lives changed profoundly. Patrick came to realize how wrong it was to kill others, and Jo began to see that perhaps if she had grown up in the environment Patrick had grown up, she too might have been led to violent acts.

The friendship between Jo and Patrick was also healing. As a result, they now travel the world together telling their stories. A play called "The Bomb" has been written about them. Often Patrick and Jo conduct workshops after the play is performed.

Today they are a two-person team traveling throughout the world for peace. They want the world to know that from tragedy can come something good.

The story of Jo and Patrick is not unique by any means. In fact, there are many movements throughout the world in which two sides have come together for mutual understanding, forgiveness, and friendship. We hear of Israelis and Palestinians working together for peace. We hear of Protestants and Catholics in Northern Ireland coming together in peace. We hear of Christians of different denominations working together on projects to benefit humanity. The list is long, very long.

Today's story from Jesus, however, is about more than forgiveness. That is simply the element I have chosen to discuss in this homily.

The other element in the story is that of self-righteousness or judging others. Jesus condemned judging others. He condemned this evil not only in this story, but on other occasions. He reminded his disciples, for example, that before finding the little fault in others—which he called "the speck in another's eye"—his disciples should first work on getting rid of the big faults—which he called "the planks in their own eyes." He commanded us not to judge, that we not be judged.

Forgiveness and not being judgmental are both Christian commandments. However, they are both very difficult. Perhaps that is why we never hear people rising up demanding that those commandments be carved into marble and put in front of courthouses or outside of church buildings. After all, our children would see them, and they might begin to question why we don't like to follow them.

As we continue our life journeys this week, it would be a good idea to reflect on how good we are in forgiving others, and how good we are in avoiding judgment of others.

And that is the good news I have for you on this Fifth Sunday of Lent.

Story source: Jo Berry and Pat Magee, *The Forgiveness Project*, WWW, March 29, 2010.

Chapter 14

Palm Sunday - C
Holy Week

Scripture:

- Isaiah 50: 4-7
- Psalm 22: 8-9, 17-18a, 19-20, 23-24
- Philippians 2: 6-11
- Luke 22: 14 – 23: 56

Today we begin the most special week of the year for Christians, Holy Week.

Palm Sunday of the Lord's Passion heralds the beginning of this special week. When we hear the Passion according to St. Luke, we read not only the great welcome he received from the people, but we then learn how they turned against him.

During Holy Week, people celebrate the annual Chrism Mass. At that Mass, the bishops and priests will renew their priestly promises, and they will bless the three oils that will go to each parish for the coming year. The priests and bishops will use the oils to celebrate sacraments such as Baptism, Confirmation, Sacrament of the Sick, and Holy Orders.

On Holy Thursday, Catholic Christians will celebrate a special Mass called the Mass of the Lord's Supper. As the Mass begins, the Season of Lent officially ends, and we enter a three-day Season called Triduum. At this Mass, the people will bring the three oils blessed at the Chrism Mass to the priest, and the priest will wash the feet of some people just as Jesus washed the feet of the Twelve Apostles. The washing of the feet symbolizes the new form of leadership Jesus gave to his disciples: that is, to be the leader, one must be the servant of all.

On Good Friday, we commemorate Jesus' Passion and Death. The traditional Catholic Good Friday service is in three parts: Reading of the Passion; Veneration of the Cross; and a Communion Service. In American parishes blessed with vibrant Hispanic communities, a live *Vía Crucis*, or Way of the Cross," will be held.

On Holy Saturday, Catholic Christians celebrate the most elaborate Mass of the year, the Easter Vigil Mass. At this celebration, we will have the Blessing of the New Fire, Blessing of the New Water, Blessing of the Easter Candle, and most importantly, we celebrate Sacraments of Initiation for people coming into the Catholic Church.

Easter Sunday is considered the highest feast day of the year for Catholic Christians. In fact, it is so important that we commemorate Sunday as the Lord's Day, replacing the Sabbath (Saturday) as the day of rest.

Catholic Christians are encouraged to attend as many of the Holy Week celebrations as possible.

And that is the good news I have for you on this Palm Sunday.

Chapter 15

Easter - C
Easter and the Parish

Scripture:

- Acts 10: 34a, 37-43
- Psalm 118: 1-2, 16-17, 22-23
- 1 Corinthians 5: 6b-8
- John 20: 1-9

On behalf of the staff, faculty, and the thousands of anointed ministers of our parish, I wish you and those you love a most Blessed Easter. I pray that the Holy Spirit will touch your hearts in a very special way this sacred season and give you renewed faith, hope, love, and joy.

In our part of the world, Easter falls in spring. At this time of year, it seems that all of nature celebrates Easter, for it is in a state of incredible rebirth. Trees become greener every day. Flowers spring up everywhere. Bees return to their work of pollinating and making honey, while butterflies appear once again to grace us. Birds and other animals give birth. The cycle of life continues. Nature becomes transformed.

But Easter is not just about Jesus rising from the dead. For Christians, Easter is also about us. Like nature—God's incredible show—we too are called to join in this wonderful transformation. We too are called to cast off our vices and clothe ourselves with a mantle of virtue. Like the flowers and trees that are basking in new glory, we too are called to come out of the shadows into the light. We are called to shine, to be "lights to the world" as Christ commanded us. All of us, by virtue of our baptism, are anointed ministers of the Catholic Church. That is why, when people say, "Are you alone at St. Mary's?" I reply, "No. I have about 5,000 official, anointed ministers helping me."

Catholic Christians in the United States live their faith not only in their homes, but also in their parishes. In fact, all Catholic Christians are asked to be registered members of a parish. It is in that place where we celebrate the milestones of our lives, help one another on our Faith journeys as pilgrim people, and flourish and grow.

Some people, though, fail to realize the importance of a parish. They think they can "go it alone." They also ignore the fact that their very presence in a parish community may actually help others who may need their example and wisdom. That pretty much describes the soap maker in the following story told by Norman Lawson.

One day, a rabbi and a soap maker went for a walk together. The soap maker said, "What good is religion? Look at all the trouble and misery in the world today! We still have all these problems even after thousands of years of religious leaders teaching about goodness and truth and peace. We still have all these problems despite prayers and sermons. If religion were good and true, we wouldn't have the problems we have today."

The rabbi said nothing as they continued walking. Suddenly, the rabbi noticed a child playing in a mud puddle.

The rabbi said, "Look at that child. You claim that using soap makes people clean, but see the dirt on that child? What good is soap? With all the soap in the world, over all these years, that child is still filthy. I guess soap is not very effective after all!"

The soap maker protested by saying, "But, Rabbi, soap cannot do any good unless it is used!"

The rabbi smiled and said, "Exactly! Exactly!"

This is a wonderful story to remind us that our faith is what we make of it. Likewise, our parish is what we make of it.

As you know, God is showering incredible blessings on our parish. Last evening, for example, we celebrated Sacraments of Initiation of our RCIA Ministry for over thirty-five people. Our parish continues to grow at a rapid rate, and new ministries appear on a regular basis. We have just sent one man off to the seminary to become a priest, and we have another young man studying to be a deacon. We have two women exploring the Religious Life. We continue to have many called to be lay missionaries, and we are giving them a taste of mission life by sending them to our sister parish in the mountains of Honduras. We continue serving several thousand poor people every year in our parish with food, clothing, furniture, and health care. And we continue to celebrate hundreds of baptisms, weddings, Confirmations, anniversaries, *Quinceañeras*, Presentations, and other milestones every year.

On this Easter Sunday, all of us are called to transform our lives and rededicate ourselves. I ask you to re-dedicate yourself to your parish and parish life. Get involved. Exercise your God-given ministry. For just as birds fly and fish swim, ministers are supposed to do ministry. God will bless you beyond your wildest imagination!

And that is the good news I have for you on this Easter Sunday.

Story source: "Doubting Thomas," in Gerard Fuller (Ed.), *Stories for All Seasons,* Mystic, CT: Twenty-Third Publications, 1996, pp. 102-103. Based on Norm Lawson's, "Faith" in *The Pastor's Professional Research Service,* RS 7, 89-8-89-1.

Chapter 16

2nd Sunday of Easter – C
Doubt and Resurrection

Scripture:

- Acts 5: 12-16
- Psalm 118: 2-4, 13-15, 22-24
- Revelation 1: 9-11a, 12-13, 17-19
- John 20: 19-31

On this Second Sunday of Easter, also known as Divine Mercy Sunday, we once again encounter the story of Thomas. In this story, his fellow apostles told Thomas that Jesus had been raised from the dead and had appeared to them. But because Thomas was absent on the day that Jesus had appeared to the others, he expressed serious doubts. Ever since that day, poor Thomas has become known as "Doubting Thomas."

This story is very important, for it brings up the idea of doubt. I think just about everyone, including religious leaders, has some doubts about some parts of their Faith from time to time. That is exactly what we see in the following story about two traveling missionaries.

These missionaries belonged to a religious cult that believed that it alone possessed "the truth" about Jesus. Anyone who did not believe as they did, they thought, was wrong.

To spread their beliefs, they traveled the country visiting churches, especially little ones. Once they got into the church, they would begin telling the pastor and congregation about how they alone possessed "the truth" about Jesus. Because they were so arrogant, they were rather obnoxious. Therefore, they had a very difficult time making converts.

One day, they found a little church where a minister was alone working on his homily for the upcoming Sunday. After telling the minister how they alone possessed "the truth" about Jesus, they told the minister that faith was everything. They told him that if he believed as fully as they did, he could even drink poison and it would not harm him.

After listening to the missionaries for a while, the minister said, "Okay, I'll make a deal with you. I have a glass of poison here. If you will drink this poison and remain alive, I'll join your religious group. But if you don't drink this poison, I'll have to conclude that you are false ministers of the Gospel, because surely your Lord wouldn't allow you to perish."

The cult missionaries were now in a bind. What should they do? Should they drink the poison, or should they flee the scene? They decided to discuss their dilemma. After a few minutes, they came back to the minister and said, "We've decided on another plan. You drink the poison, and we'll raise you from the dead."

I love this story, for it shows that even persons who believe their faith is rock-solid can have doubts. If the cult missionaries truly believed in what they were preaching, they would have drunk the poison immediately. But as it turned out, they had doubts.

Stories like that of Thomas and that of the cult missionaries force us to look at our own faith life. To do that, it would be a good idea to look at the concept of doubt. Here are three points to keep in mind.

First, everyone has doubts from time to time, and that is good. An unquestioned faith is less powerful than one that has been examined. Doubts, in the context we're talking about today, refer to uncertainties. If someone tells you they never have uncertainties about their faith, be very suspicious. The famous philosopher and social critic of the last century, Bertrand Russell, said, "The whole problem with the world is that fools and fanatics are always so certain of themselves, but wiser people so full of doubts."

Second, whether we believe in various things does not affect how God cares for us. God is on duty twenty-four hours a day, seven days a week. That is one of the reasons that Catholic Christians celebrate Eucharist every day. We want to show our gratitude to God for watching over us. Our particular beliefs – and doubts – will not change God's love and protection of us.

Babies, for example, have no idea about cars, driver safety, and the like. Though they totally lack knowledge of these things, they are transported safely from point A to point B by their parents in a car. It is the parents who have to know what they're doing, not the infants. That is how God works in our lives. God runs the universe, and how God runs the universe does not depend on our particular belief systems. I'm sure that is big news for those of us who, from time to time, like to be "control freaks."

Finally, like all our problems, one solution to doubt is to turn it over to God. St. Ignatius of Loyola, the great founder of the Society of Jesus, had a prayer about this: "Lord, help me in my unbelief."

In this simple prayer, Ignatius showed two important things. First, this spiritual giant showed that he had enough self-awareness to recognize he had "unbelief." Second, he knew that God could help him with this difficulty. What a beautiful concept this is!

As we continue our life journey this week, it would be a good idea to examine our own faith. What kinds of doubts do we have? Have we ever considering handing them over to God?

And that is the good news I have for you on this Second Sunday of Easter.

Story source: Author unknown.

Chapter 17

3rd Sunday of Easter – C
Feed the Sheep Here

Scripture:

- Acts 5: 27-32, 40b-41
- Psalm 30: 2 & 4, 5-6, 11& 12a & 13b
- Revelation 5: 11-14
- John 21: 1-19

On this Third Sunday of Easter, we hear about two images or symbols that Jesus used to describe his followers. The first image is that of the fish, one of the earliest symbols of our Church. Jesus was trying to teach the disciples that through their own efforts, they would be unsuccessful, but when they had the Lord's help, they could accomplish miracles. To demonstrate this, he had the disciples go fishing at his command. In spite of having caught no fish during the night, with Jesus' help they caught many fish.

The second image Jesus used for humanity was that of sheep. He told Peter to "feed my sheep." This command is taken to refer not just to Peter, whom Catholic Christians consider to have been the first pope of the Church, but also to all priests. And because every Catholic Christian becomes part of the "priesthood of all believers" at his or her baptism, Jesus' command to feed his flock refers to us all.

In the following story, we see how one man fed his flock in many ways.

There was once a blacksmith who worked very hard at his trade. When it was his turn to die, an angel came to him to bring him to God. Much to the angel's surprise, the blacksmith refused to go. The blacksmith told the angel to go back to God and tell him that he was the only blacksmith in the area, and he was needed on Earth because all his neighbors needed him for the planting and sowing season. So, the angel told God that the blacksmith was a very good man: he didn't want to appear ungrateful for having a place in the kingdom, but wished he could remain on Earth and help his neighbors. God granted the blacksmith's request.

A year or two went by, and the angel returned to the blacksmith to tell him that the Lord was ready to share the fullness of the kingdom with him. Once again, though, the blacksmith was not ready to go. He told the angel that he had a neighbor who was seriously ill, and it was time for the harvest. Therefore, the blacksmith agued, it would be better for him to stay on Earth to help the other neighbors bring in the ill man's crops. After all, the blacksmith argued, he did not want the ill man and his family to become destitute because they could not bring in the crops. Once again, the angel left the blacksmith alone.

Through the years, the blacksmith and angel got into a pattern. The angel would come to the blacksmith, and the blacksmith would come up with one reason or another why he was too busy to go to heaven right then.

Finally, the blacksmith grew very old and very tired. He finally decided that it was time to go to the Lord. Therefore, he prayed, "God, if you'd like to send your angel again, I'd be glad to come home now." Immediately the angel appeared to the blacksmith at the speed of light. The blacksmith said, "Hello, angel, if you still want to take me home, I'm ready to live forever in the kingdom of heaven." The angel laughed and laughed and laughed and looked at the blacksmith with delight and surprise in his eyes and said, "My friend. Where do you think you've been all these years?! You have been in the kingdom of heaven!"

The blacksmith had been at home with the Lord all that time.

This beautiful story, along with the Gospel message of the fish and sheep, reminds of us of three things.

First, the kingdom of God is at hand. It is literally at hand. While the perfect state of the kingdom of God is in the afterlife, it begins here. Thus, we are part of this kingdom right here and right now. Our call to holiness is now, right here on Earth. We are called to serve the Lord in building up the kingdom by serving others in need. That is exactly what the blacksmith was doing all along.

Second, each one of us is a priest by virtue of our baptism. Though the "priesthood of all believers" is different in both degree and kind from the ordained priesthood, it is the bedrock of the Church. Most adults exercise their priesthood by becoming heads of the domestic church, the family. Their sheep are their children. As priests, they must "feed" their flock just as Peter was called to do. They do this by teaching their children basic values, telling them stories of Jesus and God and his awesome creation, telling them stories from the Bible, showing them how to read and treasure the Bible, teaching them about the symbols of our Faith and how to celebrate rituals in the home, and teaching them how to pray. They also do this by bringing them to the parish, also known as the second level of Church, for faith formation and celebration of sacraments. The priests of the domestic church—dads and moms, godfathers and godmothers, grandmothers and grandfathers, aunts and uncles, even older brothers and sisters—have very heavy responsibilities.

And finally, we learn that our call as followers of Jesus is a servant call. We are called to be humble servants of Jesus Christ. And where is Jesus? He lives in every human being we encounter on our life journey. There are no exceptions to this rule. Therefore, how we treat others is how we treat Christ.

As we continue our life journey this week, it would be good to ask ourselves how we live our own priesthood. How do we "feed" our flock?

And that is the good news I have for you on this Third Sunday of Easter.

Story source: "The Blacksmith," in William J. Bausch (Ed.), *World of Stories for Preachers and Teachers,* Mystic, CT: Twenty-Third Publications, 1998, #113, p. 264.

Chapter 18

4th Sunday of Easter – C
St. Margaret Clitherow

Scripture:

- Acts 13: 14, 43-52
- Psalm 100: 1-2, 3, 5
- Revelation 7: 9, 14b-17
- John 10: 27-30

Last Sunday as we gathered to celebrate Eucharist, we heard Jesus telling Peter to "feed his sheep." Today, we hear Jesus say that his sheep, or followers, hear his voice and follow him. As a result, they will never perish.

For more than two thousand years now, Catholic Christians have tried to follow Jesus in many ways. One of the most important of these is to celebrate the Eucharist, or Mass, as he commanded us to do. As you may remember, on the night before he was crucified, he celebrated the Passover dinner with his disciples. During the dinner, he took bread, broke it, gave it to his disciples, and said, "Take this, all of you, and eat of it, for this is my Body, which will be given up for you." He then took a cup of wine and said, "Take this, all of you, and drink from it, for this is the chalice of my Blood, the Blood of the new and eternal covenant, which will be poured out for you and for many for the forgiveness of sins." He then gave his disciples this command: "Do this in memory of me."

This "Last Supper" is considered by Catholic Christians to be the first Mass and the beginning of the ordained priesthood. We believe that through the ages, ordained priests are commanded by Jesus to ask God the Father to send down God the Holy Spirit to change the bread and wine into the Body and Blood of Jesus Christ. When they do this, Catholic Christians then follow the command of Jesus to eat and drink.

Unfortunately, though, not everyone has loved this most precious gift of Jesus. In fact, in many times and in many places, people have tried to prevent the Mass from being celebrated. They have done this by killing priests, outlawing the Mass from being celebrated, or outlawing Christ's Church. Despite all the efforts to stamp out the Mass, though, it has lived. There have always been people brave enough to protect it from its enemies. One such person was Margaret of York, sometimes called "The Pearl of York."

Margaret Medleton was born in York, England around 1556. When she was fifteen years old, she married a Protestant man by the name of John Clitherow. John and Margaret had three children together. When Margaret was eighteen years old, she became a Catholic Christian. At this time, that was a very dangerous thing to do, as the Queen had banned the Catholic Church as well as the Mass and Catholic priests. John, even though he did not agree with his wife's faith, was very tolerant. In fact, he allowed her to raise the three children as Catholic Christians.

Knowing that Holy Communion could not exist without the Mass, Margaret began a ministry of hiding Catholic priests as well as their vestments and other items needed to celebrate Mass. Many times she would be arrested, but that never stopped her.

Finally, though, on March 25, 1586, Margaret was executed for her faith by being crushed to death with a door and stones. Her two sons became Catholic priests, and her daughter became a Religious Sister.

Margaret was canonized in 1970 as, "St. Margaret of York." Quite correctly, she is known as a "Martyr of the Eucharist."

Now, more than two thousand years after Jesus gave us the command to celebrate the Mass and consume his Body and Blood, and more than four hundred years after the martyrdom of St. Margaret of York, our parish community comes together to witness many children celebrating their First Communion at our weekend Masses. In time, God willing, they will grow up to witness their own children and grandchildren doing the same thing. Christ's message lives, and it will not be destroyed. Thanks be to God!

Of all the things a parish priest does during the year, perhaps nothing is as joyful as watching precious young people receive Jesus in the Blessed Sacrament for the first time.

For those making their First Communion, I say congratulations! I ask that you always stay close to Jesus in the Blessed Sacrament. Jesus gave us no more precious gift than himself. As long as you stay close to Jesus in the Blessed Sacrament, you will always be able to weather the storms of life that you will experience.

For the adults here today who may not be able to receive Communion, I ask that you consider coming to see me. Maybe there is some obstacle that is barring you from receiving Holy Communion. If so, together we can knock down the barrier. It might take us a long time and a lot of work, but so what? Isn't Jesus Christ worth it? Of course he is!

So as we continue our celebration today, we do so with hearts filled with joy and hope. May God bless you all, and may God be praised for giving us his Son.

And that is the good news I have for you on this Fourth Sunday of Easter.

Story source: "St. Margaret Clitherow," in *Butler's Lives of the Saints: New Full Edition: March*, Revised by Teresa Rodriguez, Collegeville, MN: The Liturgical Press/ Burns & Oates, 1999, pp. 248-253.

Chapter 19

5th Sunday of Easter – C
Victor Learns to Love

Scripture:

- Acts 14: 21-27
- Psalm 145: 8-9, 10-11, 12-13ab
- Revelation 21: 1-5a
- John 13: 31-33a, 34-35

As we come together to celebrate Eucharist today, we hear Jesus tell his disciples to love one another. In fact, he said that how they love one another is how people would be able to tell that they were his disciples.

But the English language is very ambiguous when it comes to love. Sociologists, for example, have identified at least six different kinds of love. The type Jesus commanded us to embrace is known as *agape* or altruistic love. It is a type of love that at its best is completely unselfish and characterized by unconditional caring, nurturing, giving, forgiving, and self-sacrificing for others. In other words, we wish the best for others, unconditionally. So it does not matter if we like the other person or if they like us and treat us well. We are to wish the very best for others— no strings attached. That is what the young man in the following story learned the hard way.

There was once a young woman who gave birth to her first child just one month after her husband had died in an accident. Her friends and neighbors were very sad about the death of the woman's husband, so they gave her a shower to help her get started. At the shower, the young mother received many beautiful presents for her and the baby, whom she decided to name Victor after her deceased husband.

After everyone had left the shower, the young widow received a visit from Doc Burns, a little old man who lived alone in a house at the corner of the street. Nobody ever talked much to him, though he often waved to people as they walked by his humble house.

"I have come to give you my gift for your young son," he said. "I have come to offer to grant you one wish for young Victor. However, you must make the wish before he is baptized on Sunday." The little man bowed and walked back to his house.

The young mother was baffled by the words of the strange little man. Did he really have the power to grant a wish? What should she ask for? All week long she could not make up her mind. Finally, just before the Baptism, the mother asked for the wish. "I wish that everyone in the world will always love my Victor."

And the wish came true. Victor grew up to be a very handsome young man. As a toddler, people could not resist hugging and touching him. Even when he was naughty, no one could believe that he had done anything wrong. As he grew older, Victor became known and loved in the village. Even the other children were always giving Victor toys and food. If the mother punished Victor, all the other adults would come to his aid. Although the people seemed to adore him, Victor responded to all the attention he received with scorn and contempt. The only one he ever listened to was Doc Burns.

When Victor graduated from high school, he received a scholarship to a fine university in the eastern United States. At Christmas, when he returned home for a visit for the first time, he drove up in a beautiful black Cadillac. His trunks were filled with fine clothes, and he had plenty of spending money. He seldom saw his mother during the vacation. Instead, he spent his nights out drinking at parties and taverns.

After college, Victor never had to work for a living because his friends continued to support him. Women smothered him with attention, and his friends raved about him. Nevertheless, his heart grew empty and his soul grew sick. He despised people who catered to him. He became disgusted with everything and everyone.

One night, Victor mixed a glass of poison to kill himself. But suddenly Doc Burns appeared and took the glass from Victor. When he learned that Victor saw his life as meaningless, Doc Burns said, "I suppose it is partially my fault. When you were baptized, I granted your mother a wish for you, that everyone in the world would always love you. Suppose I grant you a new wish. What would it be?"

Victor, after much soul-searching, said, "Take away the old magic and give me a new wish. Rather than being loved, I ask for the ability to love everyone in the world." Doc Burns granted the wish and said, "Now, Victor, things will go better for you."

Things did go better for Victor, but not immediately. Without his great charm, Victor was abandoned by many of his friends. Several people retaliated for the past wrongs he had afflicted on them. He was thrown in jail for three months, and no one came to visit him. When he was released, he was sick, lonely, and penniless.

Victor returned home to find his mother very ill, and for the first time in his life, he was able to return her great love. When his mother was well, Victor took a job as a school janitor. He not only cared for the building, but also for the children, particularly those who came from poor homes. To all the children he became "Mr. Victor," their friend and companion.

Finally, he met a beautiful young widow who had two small children. They married, and he gave all three of them the love that they so desperately needed. Though he was poor in possessions, Victor was one of the richest men in the world. He discovered that it was in loving, not in being loved, that life comes to its fullest expression.

For those of you receiving their First Communion today, I say Congratulations. May Jesus grant you the ability to love people unconditionally, all the days of your lives.

And that is the good news I have for you on this Fifth Sunday of Easter.

Story source: "Victor," in William J. Bausch (Ed.), *A World of Stories for Preachers and Teachers,* Mystic, CT: Twenty-Third Publications, 1998, #5, pp. 23-25.

Chapter 20

6th Sunday of Easter – C
Peace and Marriage Tips

Scripture:

- Acts 15: 1-2, 22-29
- Psalm 67: 2-3, 5, 6 & 8
- Revelation 21: 10-14, 22-23
- John 14: 23-29

On this Sixth Sunday of Easter, we hear Jesus telling his disciples, before ascending into heaven, "My peace I leave with you; my peace I give to you" (John 14: 27).

"Peace," in Catholic Christian theology, does not refer to the absence of war. Rather, it refers to things being in harmony with God's will. As we recall, the early human beings sinned against God, and that caused disharmony to reign over the world. Because it was God who was offended by the sins of our ancestors, God promised that he would send a savior to make reparation. This savior, as we discovered, turned out be both fully human and fully divine. The Savior was none other than God the Son, known in the earthly realm as Jesus of Nazareth.

A human-divine Savior was most appropriate. After all, it was humans who destroyed the beauty God had created for them. But it was God who was offended. Therefore, having a Savior who was both human and God was the perfect Being to make reparation, to bring peace or harmony back into the God-human relationship.

But the peace of Christ is something we Christians are called to mimic. We, too, are called to be people of harmony. We do this by loving one another as Christ loved us.

One of the first places we practice this harmony is in the home.

Many people through the ages have presented tips or suggestions on how to have this peace or harmony in the home. Today I present seventeen tips or "rules" for a happy marriage given by a writer named Roy Burgess.

"17 Rules for a Happy Marriage"

1. The very nearest approach to domestic happiness on each side is the cultivation on both sides of absolute unselfishness.
2. Never both be angry at once.
3. Never speak loudly to one another unless the house is on fire.
4. Let each one strive to yield most often to the wishes of the other.
5. Let self-denial be the daily aim and practice of each partner.
6. Never find fault unless it is perfectly certain that fault has been committed, and always speak lovingly.
7. Never taunt with past mistakes.
8. Neglect the whole world rather than one another.

9. Never allow a request to be repeated.
10. Never part for a day without loving words to think of during the absence.
11. Never make a remark at the expense of each other.
12. Never let the sun go down on any anger or grievance.
13. Never meet without a loving welcome.
14. Never forget the happy hours of early love.
15. Never sigh over what might have been, but make the best of what is.
16. Never forget that marriage is ordained of God, and that His blessings alone can make it what it should be.
17. Never be content till you know both are walking in the same narrow path.

From this list, and from Jesus' call to peace, we can learn many things. Here are just three.

First, peace is possible. We can enter harmonious relationships with God and with other human beings.

Second, peace requires work. If peace were always easy, there would be no conflict in this world. Everything and everybody would be in harmony.

And third, the call for peace begins with us in our own lives. While we are grateful that we have ambassadors and other government officials trying to create harmony among the nations of the world, we ordinary people must be ambassadors of peace in our own homes and workplaces.

As we continue our life journeys this week, it would be a good idea to take some time to reflect on how well we are living in peace and harmony with those around us.

And that is the good news I have for you on this Sixth Sunday of Easter.

Story source: Roy Burgess, "17 Rules for a Happy Marriage," in Brian Cavanaugh (Ed.), *Sower's Seeds that Nurture Family Values: Sixth Planting,* New York: Paulist Press, 2000, #73, pp. 79-80.

Chapter 21

Ascension - C
Yesterday and Today

Scripture:

- Acts 1: 1-11
- Psalm 47: 2-3, 6-7, 8-9
- Ephesians 1: 17-23
- Luke 24: 46-53

Today we celebrate the Feast of the Ascension. This day commemorates Jesus rising to heaven after spending some time on Earth after his resurrection from the dead.

Before rising to heaven, Jesus promised his disciples that the Holy Spirit would be coming upon them, and then they would be missionaries, spreading the good news of Jesus throughout the whole world. That event, which we will celebrate next week, is called Pentecost, the birthday of the Church.

Imagine all the emotions the early disciples must have experienced at that time. First, the man they followed was crucified and buried, then he rose from the dead and began appearing to them and teaching them, and now he is leaving once again. Unlike us, they did not have two thousand years of history and theology to fall back on to make sense out of any of this. Many of them must have been afraid and wondering. Would God really come to them? Would they be okay? Without Jesus, were they safe?

Like those early disciples, we too often have conflicting emotions. We too are often fearful in our everyday life. One wise man, by the name of Robert J. Burdette, examined life and decided that there were two days of the week that he was going to consider carefree days, days free from fear and apprehension. Those two days were yesterday and tomorrow. Here is what he wrote:

> "There are two golden days in the week which I never worry about—two carefree days kept sacredly free from fear and apprehension.
>
> "One of those days is yesterday. Yesterday, with all its cares and frets, all its pains and aches, all its faults, its mistakes and blunders, has passed forever beyond recall. I cannot unsay a word once said. All that it holds of my life—of wrong, of regret and sorrow—is in the hands of the Mighty Love that can bring honey out of the rock and the sweetest water out of the bitterest desert. Save for the beautiful memories, sweet and tender, that linger like the perfume of roses in the heart of the day that is gone, I have nothing to do with yesterday. It was mine. It is God's now.
>
> And the other day that I do not worry about is tomorrow. Tomorrow, with all its possible adversities, its perils, its large

promise and poor performance, its failures and mistakes, is as far beyond my mastery as its dead sister, yesterday. It's God's day. Its sun will rise in splendor or behind a mass of clouds, but it will rise.

Until then, the same love and patience that held yesterday, holds tomorrow. Save for the star of hope and faith that gleams forever on the brow of tomorrow, shining with tender promise into the heart of today, I have no possession in that unborn day of grace. Tomorrow is God's day. It will be mine.

There is left for myself, then, but one day in the week—today! And you can fight the battles of today. Any person can resist temptation for just one day. Any man or woman can carry the burdens for just one day. It is only when we willfully add the burdens of those awful eternities, yesterday and tomorrow—such burdens as only the mighty God can sustain—that we break down. It isn't the experience of today that drives people mad, it is the remorse of something that happened yesterday, and the dread of what tomorrow brings. Those are God's days; leave them with God.

Therefore, I think and I do and I journey, but one day at a time. That is my day. Dutifully, I run my course and work my appointed task on that day of mine; and God, the Almighty and All-loving, takes care of yesterday and tomorrow."

When we encounter inspirational pieces of writing on the folly of fretting about yesterday or worrying about tomorrow, we realize how true it is. On the other hand, we know how difficult it is to completely let go of yesterday and to not worry about tomorrow.

As for yesterday, we can thank God today for the many blessings He showered on us that day. We can also learn from the mistakes of yesterday and promise to do better today. As for tomorrow, we prepare for it by living today as best we can. When it comes right down to it, we never have more than today. Are we living today with full gusto and enthusiasm and joy?

And that is the good news I have for you on the Feast of the Ascension.

Story source: Robert J. Burdette, "Two Golden Days," in Brian Cavanaugh (Ed.), *Sower's Seeds Aplenty: Fourth Planting,* New York: Paulist Press, 1996, #46, pp. 34-35.

Chapter 22

Pentecost - C
The Dark Lantern

Scripture:

- Acts 2: 1-11
- Psalm 104; 1ab & 24ac, 29bc-30, 31 & 34
- 1 Corinthians 12: 3b-7, 12-13
- John 20: 19-23

Today we celebrate the Feast of Pentecost, the day the Holy Spirit came upon the early disciples, bringing gifts of courage and enthusiasm and zeal. Of all the feast days of the Church, none is more associated with wild excitement than this feast.

But the disciples did not simply receive these gifts. Rather, they put these gifts into action by becoming missionaries. They didn't just jump around praising God. On the contrary, they left their homes to spread the good news of Jesus Christ throughout the whole world. That is why this Feast is called the Birthday of the Catholic Church in particular, and Christianity in general.

The story of Pentecost shows us that simply possessing gifts is not enough; we need to put them into action. That is something that is reflected in the following story by author Les Christie.

Many years ago, in a small American town, there was a man whose job it was to watch a railroad crossing during the night. When a train was approaching, his job was to wave a lantern to warn cars on the narrow road to stop until the train went by.

One night, as a train was approaching the railroad crossing, the man took his place to warn oncoming cars. He could see a car in the distance approaching the railroad tracks, so he began to wave his lantern. The car, though, kept on coming, so the man waved his lantern even more forcefully. The train was only seconds away, but the car did not even slow down. Waving the lantern as fast as he could was futile. The car sped onto the railroad tracks just as the train was crossing. The car was demolished, and everyone in the car was killed.

At the investigation of the accident, the grief-stricken man explained to the authorities how he had tried to warn the oncoming car, but the driver of the car did not stop. The officer in charge of the investigation said, "Sir, you indeed did wave your lantern—however, you forgot to light it, so nobody saw it in the darkness of the night!"

What a sad, sad story this is. Many of us might be thinking to ourselves how stupid it was, forgetting to light the lantern. After all, what good is a man waving a lantern at night if it isn't lit?

But that is exactly what some of us do in our daily lives, and there is no better time to reflect on two types of mistakes Christians can make than on the Feast of Pentecost.

The first mistake is to have many gifts but fail to use them. I have personally known people with astonishing abilities who simply ignore them. I know a young man, for example, who went to four years of university to obtain his bachelor's degree, two years to do his philosophy and religious studies requirements, one year of pastoral experience, and four years of theology—all to become a Catholic priest. After being a priest for a year, he decided he would rather be something different. Eleven years of study down the drain. I know another person who spent about the same amount of time becoming a physician. When she was finished, she decided she would rather stay at home.

Now everyone must walk the path God has called him or her to, so I certainly don't want to judge these two persons. Only they know God's will for them. But I use them simply to reflect on those who have so many gifts but do not share them with those who could use them. What good are faith and intelligence and energy and love if they are not put into action?

When I talk about putting one's faith into action, I'm not necessarily talking about people doing heroic things for their faith. I'm also talking about simple things. I'm talking about inviting people to Mass or to your parish. I'm talking about being generous stewards of your time, talent, and treasure. I'm talking about becoming less self-centered and becoming more other-centered.

The second mistake some people make is trying to be workers without having the necessary internal gifts. These folks might be compared to the dark lantern swinging in the night: very active, but nothing inside. I remember one person, for example, who went on a mission trip to a foreign land. He was there for about a week, and when he came home he decided that his purpose in life was to "organize" the people in this mission land. Never mind that he could not speak their language. Never mind that he could not hold a job. Never mind that the other lay missionaries said they would never again go on a mission trip if he also went. He didn't have a clue. He wanted to be a person of action, but he did not possess the necessary gifts to make the actions work.

We need not only the gifts the Spirit brings us at our baptism, but we need to develop them and then share them abundantly with others. That is what being a missionary means—and all of us are called to be missionaries—whether we are missionaries in Wilmington, North Carolina or Honduras or India or Peru or wherever else our parish's lay missionaries are serving.

How are you using the gifts the Holy Spirit gave you to serve Christ in others?

And that is the good news I have for you on this Feast of Pentecost.

Story source: Les Christie, "The Lantern," in Wayne Rice (Ed.), *More Hot Illustrations for Youth Talks,* Grand Rapids, MI: Youth Specialties/Zondervan, 1995, p. 104.

Part Three

ORDINARY TIME

Chapter 23

Holy Trinity – C
Imitating the Trinity

Scripture:

- Proverbs 8: 22-31
- Psalm 8: 4-5, 6-7, 8-9
- Romans 5: 1-5
- John 16: 12-15

This weekend we celebrate the Feast of the Most Holy Trinity in the Catholic Church, a day when we remember the three Persons in One God.

The concept of the Trinity is unique to Christianity. As we learned as children, this concept is a total mystery, human beings can never understand it. However, just because we cannot understand it with our puny human minds, God has inspired spiritual writers throughout the centuries to record glimpses or hints about the Trinity's nature.

For example, the Religious Sisters I had as childhood teachers told us of how St. Patrick used a shamrock to talk about the Trinity. Just as there are three leaves on a shamrock but only one shamrock, there are three Persons but only one God.

We also learned that the three Persons were named the Father, Son, and Holy Spirit—although when I was growing up, the Holy Spirit was called the Holy Ghost. Further, we learned that each of the Persons had different jobs to do.

When I grew up and went to seminary, I learned that writers throughout the ages had written volumes and volumes of books and articles about the Trinity, despite the fact that it is a mystery.

One thing that was never covered, though, was how we human beings are called to model or imitate the Trinity. We have heard about "imitating Christ," which refers to modeling Jesus. But how do we model the whole Trinity? After all, are we not created in the "image of God?" Of course we are. Therefore, we should know how to model God.

God the Father, as we know, is the Creator of the universe including us human beings. As the documents of the Second Vatican Council tell us, human beings are called to be "co-creators" with God the Father. In other words, we are called to use our creative selves to create a better world.

We "co-create" when we do our jobs, when we produce and raise children, when we protect the environment as God commanded us to do, when we produce beauty through our hobbies, when we take care of our bodies. We do this when we uncover God's awesome creation through science and through our writings and art.

God the Father is also the one who forgives us when we ask. To model Him, then, we must learn to forgive others, forever holding mercy to be a superior value compared to judgment and vengeance.

Finally, God is the one who gives us our "daily bread," that is, who gives us the things we need to sustain ourselves. To model God the Father, then, we need to provide the necessities of life to those in need.

God the Son, Jesus Christ, is the Savior or Redeemer. We model Jesus when we continue his work in building what is known as the Kingdom of God here on Earth. We are called the Church or Body of Christ. This Kingdom of God includes the Church, but it is much larger. We build it by performing the corporal and spiritual works of mercy. For example, because we are called to be the hands and ears and eyes and mouth and heart of Jesus, we continue his work by comforting the sorrowful, and by giving drink to the thirsty, food to the hungry and clothes to the naked. We do this by visiting those in prison, caring for the sick, and spreading the good news of Jesus. We also model Christ when we fight against social sins such as bigotry, prejudice, discrimination, poverty, killing, hunger, violence, greed, hatred, and selfishness. We model Christ by being the champions of the underdogs of society, those who are poor, powerless, and marginalized by stigma.

Finally, we model the Holy Spirit when we show wisdom in our lives. We model the Spirit when we approach life filled with zeal and enthusiasm, as we saw last week in the Pentecost story.

We model the Spirit when we walk beside those in need on their life journeys. We model the Spirit when we help to form the consciences of children and teenagers, helping them distinguish between right and wrong. We model the Holy Spirit when we exhibit courage in the face of adversities of life. We model the Holy Spirit when we never give up hope no matter what "dark valleys" we find ourselves in.

In June and in July, lay missionaries will be journeying to Honduras to visit our sister parish. Part of their task is to model the Holy Spirit by capturing what they see on their travels in their minds, and then communicating that with others. Through their stories, they will try to "light on fire" the hearts and imaginations of our parish's students and parishioners. That is modeling the Holy Spirit in a very real way.

As we continue our life journeys this week, it would be a good idea to stop and examine our own lives.

How do you model God the Father? How does your life work make this a better world?

How do you model God the Son, Jesus Christ? How do you serve others in need?

And finally, how do you model the Holy Spirit? How do you light others on fire with the enthusiasm and zeal of your Faith?

And that is the good news I have for you on this Feast of the Holy Trinity.

Chapter 24

Holy Body and Blood of Christ – C
Behaving in Church

Scripture:

- Genesis 14: 18-20
- Psalm 110: 1, 2, 3, 4
- 1 Corinthians 11: 23-26
- Luke 9: 11b-17

Today the Catholic Church celebrates the Feast of the Body and Blood of Christ, formerly known as *"Corpus Christi."* On this day, we give thanks for the Blessed Sacrament, Jesus' real presence in the consecrated elements of bread and wine.

The Church Fathers of the Second Vatican Council reminded us that Jesus is present in four ways at every Eucharist or Mass: in the assembly (which is called the Body of Christ), in the presider (who is called the head of the body), in the proclaimed Scriptures, and in the consecrated bread and wine called the Blessed Sacrament.

Because Catholic Christians see the Eucharist as the "source and summit" of their spirituality, they have developed many ideas about how one should behave when celebrating Mass. Though there probably are as many ideas about this as there are Catholic Christians, I think there are two basic schools of though about how one should behave. But before I discuss each approach, I present this story for your consideration.

There was once a deacon from the seminary who was sent out to help in a beach-town parish for the summer. He was a nice enough young man, but he was rather rigid and opinionated. One very hot Sunday, he became very angry with the people who were coming to Mass in this Oceanside church. He was angry because the men didn't have on suits and ties, and he was angry that none of the women wore dresses. He was disgusted that many people wore shorts, and he was angry that some of the kids came to church with bathing suits and bare feet.

The young deacon shouted at the people and said, "Don't you have any respect for Jesus? If people came to your house for dinner, wouldn't you be offended if they allowed their children to come in bathing suits? Don't you think God is offended by the casual way you dress for church?"

The people were very surprised by the young deacon's anger, but they figured that he was young and immature and didn't understand much. Besides, they thought, didn't they come to church to worship God? Didn't that show their love for their Faith?

That evening, the wise old monsignor said to the young deacon, "You have a point, but have you ever gone to Mass in a European resort? There are hardly any people that go church at all. Here, our people come to Mass. They come to worship the Lord. They come in joy to visit their friend, Jesus Christ. They may look a little sloppy sometimes, yet I believe

God loves them in spite of how they are dressed and is thrilled to see them in church."

This is an important story, for it leads us to consider what is important and not important when we come to church. As I see it, there are two main schools of thought on how we are to behave in church.

People of the first school of thought hold views like the young deacon. They spend time judging others by the type of clothes they wear. They criticize young people who have rings in their noses or purple hair. They tend to be harsh towards their children, making sure they stay in their seats and are silent. In the suburban churches of my youth, parents would pinch and slap and shake their children to make them behave in church. I remember the tears of the children as their parents punished them Sunday after Sunday because their little bodies could not sit still for so long. And I always thought that Jesus, too, must shed tears at seeing how the little children were being treated in his home.

People of the second school of thought are much different. They not only recognize the real presence of Jesus in the Blessed Sacrament, but they recognize Jesus' real presence in the assembly. In fact, they hold the Catholic belief that the assembly is the Body of Christ. These people, therefore, greet each other with joy. They celebrate in the presence of the Lord. In my wonderful years of priesthood, I have been incredibly impressed by the Hispanic community and how beautifully they celebrate Mass. I love seeing the little children feel free to dance in the aisle to the beautiful music. They are worshiping their friend, Jesus, in the way they way they know how—with their whole selves.

And as we learned in Psychology 101, we can catch more flies with a teaspoon of honey than with a barrelful of vinegar. That is why people treated well in church as children are much more likely to be attracted to church as adults. If you don't believe me, I invite you to come to our Masses in Spanish and see the hordes of young men and women who worship every week.

I have to say that of the two approaches, I lean towards the latter. I do not believe the occasion of Mass should be a fashion show. I'm always happy to see people come to worship God whether they're wearing blue jeans or shorts or whatever. I think that Eucharistic Ministers or Lectors or Ushers ought to dress up a bit. That is simple common sense. But I also think little children, within reason, should be allowed to wander. Obviously, a child who is totally out of control should be taken outside for a bit. Simply use common sense. We come to church to worship God. We come to see Jesus, the man who loved having children climb all over him. We should show our joy and love.

Do you see Jesus in the assembly as easily as you do in the Blessed Sacrament?

And that is the good news I have for you on this Feast of the Body & Blood of Christ.

Story source: Unknown.

Chapter 25

2nd Sunday in Ordinary Time – C
Dream Your Dreams

Scripture:

- Isaiah 62: 1-5
- Psalm 96: 1-2a, 2b-3, 7-8a, 9-10a & c
- 1 Corinthians 12: 4-11
- John 2: 1-11

As we gather to celebrate the Eucharist on this Second Sunday in Ordinary Time, we hear the beautiful and very important words of St. Paul's first letter to the Corinthians:

"There are different gifts but the same Spirit; there are different ministries but the same Lord; there are different works but the same God who accomplishes all of them in everyone. To each person the manifestation of the Spirit is given for the common good" (1 Corinthians 12: 4-7).

Though we each receive different gifts, one gift we all receive is that of dreams. Unfortunately, we often ignore this important gift. We think dreams are unimportant, that they are like wisps of smoke—here now and gone in a flash.

But many people know the power of dreams in a human life. When I talk about "dreams," I'm not referring to what we experience when we are asleep. Rather, I'm talking about the dreams we have while we are awake—our visions, our desires. A very successful man, for example, was asked how he had become so successful. He replied, "I dream." He went on to say that he liked to turn his mind loose to imagine what he wanted to accomplish. Then, when he went to bed, he thought about those dreams, and during the night, he dreamed about them. When he got up in the morning, he envisioned ways to make his dreams come true. So while other people were saying, "You can't do that; it isn't possible," the man was well on his way to achieving what he wanted to do.

This man was someone who lived right here in our own St. Mary neighborhood in Wilmington, N.C. and went to school in our Tileston Center which was once a public school. His name was Woodrow Wilson, a man who became the Twenty-Eighth President of the United States. He said this:

"We grow great by dreams. All big men are dreamers. They see things in the soft haze of a spring day or in the red glow of a fireplace on a long winter's evening. Some of us let these great dreams die, but others nourish and protect them—nourish them through bad days until they bring them to the sunshine and light that always comes to those who sincerely hope that their dreams will come true."

As Christians, we must ask ourselves this question: How can our dreams be used for the common good of the Body of Christ, the Church? Here are three points to consider.

First, while dreams may bring us pleasure, they are not much good unless they are made concrete. Have you ever run into the person who says, "I really should write a book about my experiences"? They say this month after month, year after year. Yet they never actually sit down at the computer and begin writing. A book can't get published if it is never written. This applies to all our dreams. If you want to be in great physical shape, there are certain activities you need to do: eat right, exercise, get enough sleep, and the like. Likewise, if you'd like to have a career in a field, you need to go to school and get the right education.

Second, our dreams should benefit the greater community. One of the principles that we learn from the Bible and from Church teaching is that all of God's gifts are for the common good. God never gives us things to be hoarded. All of our gifts should be developed and shared with those who could benefit. That is how Christians grow spiritually and how they help the Church, the Body of Christ on Earth, grow and flourish. Imagine how sad it would be for a person to learn to be a carpenter or a plumber or a surgeon and never share those skills with other people.

And third, be aware that dreams can change through time. A young person just starting out in adulthood, for example, may have dreams of building a career and starting a family. As time goes on, and the kids are grown and out of the house, the person may have dreams of being a good grandparent or traveling.

Only as we grow older do we recognize how our changing dreams are part of God's plan for our lives. In my own life, for example, God has blessed me with many dreams and the wherewithal to make them come true. As a teenager, I dreamt of being a missionary priest. Because of various obstacles, God gave me a dream to serve others as a nurse, sociologist, university professor and writer. In looking back on my life, I realize that all of these dreams were to prepare me for a special type of priesthood as a parish priest. And now, my dreams have come full-circle as I dream of the day when I can retire and become the missionary priest I dreamt of being when I was a teenager! God is truly amazing in how he leads us and guides us through our dreams!

As we continue our life journeys this week, it would be a good idea to take some time for each of us to ask: "What kind of dreams do I have, and how am I working to make them come true?"

And that is the good news I have for you on this Second Sunday in Ordinary Time.

Story Source: Anonymous, "Grow Great by Dreams," in Brian Cavanaugh (Ed.), *Sower's Seeds That Nurture Family Values: Sixth Planting,* New York: Paulist Press, 2000, #7, pp. 12-13.

Chapter 26

3rd Sunday in Ordinary Time – C
Jumping Fleas

Scripture:

- Nehemiah 8: 2-4a, 5-6, 8-10
- Psalm 19: 8, 9, 10, 15
- 1 Corinthians 12: 12-30
- Luke 1: 1-4; 4: 14-21

As we come together to celebrate Eucharist on this Third Sunday in Ordinary Time, we hear the beautiful words of St. Paul in his first letter to the Corinthians.

In this letter, Paul tells the Christians that they are the body of Christ. Like a human body, there are many different parts. All of the parts of the body are for the good of all. It would be ridiculous for a foot, for example, to say, "Because I am not a hand I do not belong to the body" (1 Corinthians 12: 15).

Paul also admonishes the early Christians to be unified. Just as all parts of a human body must function together as a whole unit, so must the Church. And like a human body that suffers when one part of it is injured or diseased, so does the Church.

This reading goes very well with the Gospel reading showing Jesus telling the people: "The Spirit of the Lord is upon me, because he has anointed me to bring glad tidings to the poor" (Luke 4: 18).

Just as God the Father anointed Jesus, so are we at our baptism. At our baptism, the Holy Spirit comes upon us bringing us many gifts and talents. These gifts and talents are not only for us, but for the whole community. All of our gifts and talents are to be developed and shared with others. In other words, every Christian becomes an anointed minister at his or her baptism. Often we forget this.

Because I am the only ordained priest serving our parish, people sometimes say, "Are you alone here? Don't you have any help?" My answer is this: "I have approximately five thousand anointed ministers in this parish to help me." This is, of course very true, as we have approximately five thousand parishioners. People are often taken aback by this response, but when they reflect for a minute or two, they realize what I am telling them: all baptized Christians are part of the "priesthood of all believers" or "anointed ministers."

Unfortunately, many times ministers listen to Paul's passage selectively. They grasp the idea that all gifts are to be treasured, but they ignore the idea that they are to give to their maximum. Thus, they give minimally of themselves, thinking, "Well, I gave a little, and that's helping the whole Church." While it is true that little offerings do help the Church, God is asking us to stretch, not merely give the minimum. The late Mother

Teresa of Calcutta, for example, was asked by an American man, "Mother, how much should I give to the Church?" Mother Teresa replied, "Till it pinches. Till it pinches."

Sometimes people try to give their talents to the community, but they are prevented from doing so by people who are territorial and don't want others' help. That is what we see in the story of the jumping fleas.

Motivational speaker Zig Ziglar tells how flea trainers have observed a predictable habit of fleas during training. When fleas are first put in a jar, they can easily jump right out of the jar.

The training begins, though, when the lid is put on top of the jar. The fleas continue to jump, but they keep hitting their heads on the lid. As time goes on, the fleas continue to jump, but they do not jump high enough to hit their heads on the jar lid.

After a short time, the lid can be removed from the jar, and the fleas will continue to jump but not high enough to jump outside of the jar. They have been conditioned to jump just so high. This is similar to elephants that have one leg chained to a post in order to keep them from moving. Once they realize they can't get away, they stop fighting the chain. After a while, trainers can remove the chain and replace it with a simple rope, and the elephants still believe they are shackled to one spot.

People are sometimes like the fleas. Often when they have been swatted down for their efforts, they give up. Or, they give just enough to get by. Or they get so frustrated that they leave entirely. None of these choices help the body.

As Christians, we are called not just to be members of the body, but extraordinary members of the body. We are called to be vibrant and dynamic members of the body, bursting with excellent health. We are never to be body parts that are diseased or withering away.

But can everyone be a vibrant part of the Body of Christ? Yes! I remember an elderly, crippled woman in a suburb of Cleveland. As a seminarian, I visited her one-day with a priest. She was not able to move much, but she was incredibly serene and cheerful. Each day her caretaker would put her by the bay window to look out at the lawn and street. And each day, as she sat gazing out the window, she would pray the rosary for people listed in a little book she kept of people asking for her prayers.

She was a prayer warrior. Every priest and seminarian desired to be listed in her little book, for all sensed she was a particularly effective and strong member of the Body of Christ.

As we continue our life journey this week, it would be a good idea to ask ourselves how vibrant a member of Christ's body we are.

And that is the good news I have for you on this Third Sunday in Ordinary Time.

Story source: Zig Ziglar, "Jump Just So High," in Brian Cavanaugh (Ed.), *More Sower's Seeds: Second Planting,* New York: Paulist Press, 1992, #83, p. 78.

Chapter 27

4th Sunday in Ordinary Time – C
Steve's Attitude

Scripture:

- Jeremiah 1: 4-5, 17-19
- Psalm 71: 1-2, 3-4a, 5-6ab, 15ab & 17
- 1 Corinthians 12: 31 – 13: 13
- Luke 4: 21-30

As we come together to celebrate the Eucharist today, we hear the beautiful words of St. Paul in his first letter to the Corinthians about the nature of love. The majority of brides and grooms choose this passage as part of their wedding ceremony. And because our parish has many weddings per year, we get to hear this passage frequently.

But as we have discussed before, the word "love" has many meanings in the English language. In Greek and other languages, there are different words for each type of love such as sexual love, romantic love, and charity. The love that Paul is talking about, Christian love, refers to charity, treating others as one would like to be treated. This kind of love is not based on whether or not we "like" another person. Rather, this kind of love is action based on the belief that Christ lives in each person, and that every human being is to be treated with dignity and respect. Sometimes, though, we have to change our perspectives to appreciate this. When we do readjust our minds, we can practice love more fully. That is what Steve Covey, author of the best selling book *The Seven Habits of Highly Effective People*, shows us in the following story.

One Sunday morning, Steve was riding on a subway train in New York City. Everyone was quietly reading a newspaper or sitting with their eyes closed. Then, at one stop, a young man got on with three children. After the man sat down, the children began yelling back and forth, throwing things, and grabbing newspapers from people. The children's behavior was very disruptive to the peace and quiet the passengers had been enjoying, but the father of the children did not seem to notice. Steve was becoming increasing angry with the children and could not understand why the young father did nothing.

Finally, Steve had had enough; he was very angry. In a not very friendly tone of voice he said to the young father, "Sir, your children are really disturbing a lot of people. I wonder if you could control them a bit more." The young man lifted his eyes to Steve as if coming out of a trance and said, "Oh, you're right. I guess I should do something about it. We just came from the hospital where their mother died an hour ago. I don't know what to think, and I guess the children don't know how to handle it either."

Suddenly, Steve's attitude towards the young father changed dramatically from anger to compassion. He immediately was filled with the man's pain

110

and said, "Your wife just died? I'm so sorry! Tell me about it. What can I do to help?"

Nothing on that subway car had changed. The people were the same, and the noise was the same. What did change, though, was Steve's perception. And because his perception changed, so did his behavior.

For Christians, love is the highest of all virtues. If we have every other kind of virtue, it means nothing if we do not have love. So it behooves all of us to be experts in this virtue. Unfortunately, though, we sometimes get confused.

Sometimes we mix up Christian love—sometimes called charity or *agape*—with romantic love or with "liking" other people. But Christian love is different from the emotional state called romance, and it is different from the emotions springing from liking others. Christian love refers to seeing Christ in all people and then acting accordingly. It is that simple. We don't have to "like" people to "love" them, to see Christ in them.

In the first level of church, often called "family" or "domestic church," we show Christian love in many ways. In the domestic church, romantic love and liking are often present along with Christian love. Therefore, it is sometimes easier to help family members because we like them.

In the second level of church, which Catholic Christians call "parish," we practice our Christian love through worshipping together and by giving our time, talent, and treasure to serve each other and the needy in our local community.

The third level of church is called, in Catholic terminology, "the local church" or "diocese." And the fourth level of church is called the universal church.

In our diocese, the Bishop's Annual Appeal is a six-month period going from February to July. The funds raised in this campaign are used by the bishop to fund ministries such as campus ministry, seminarian education, catechist formation, Catholic school development, Hispanic ministry, deacon formation, Catholic Charities, African- American ministry, and many other ministries such as the North Carolina Home Mission Society that helps build churches for very poor and small new parish communities. Without our help, the bishop could not serve us as effectively as he does.

Each year, the Bishop's Annual Appeal has a particular financial goal. Each parish, in turn, is given a goal based on how much offertory it raised during the past year. For example, if our parish offertory were 2% of all the offertory collections of all the parishes in the diocese, then our BAA goal would be 2% of the total BAA goal. Our parish goal is over $122,000 for this year. That is a great increase over last year's goal of $88,000 our parish had one of the greatest increases in offertory of any parish in the diocese. The good news, though, is that our generous parishioners pledged more money last year than this year's goal. So, we should be in good shape if we all do our part.

Like last year, I'm asking you to consider a minimum pledge of $13.50 per week for six months. In other words, it would be $50 per month or $350 for the whole campaign. Many of you can do much more. I will do triple what I ask of you.

Before you make your pledge, ask yourself if you're going to go to bed hungry tonight. Will you be warm enough? Will you even have a bed and a house? If so, please be generous. Be assured that God will bless you abundantly. And if God fails to bless you sufficiently during the campaign, please see me and I'll be sure you get your money back.

And that is the good news I have for you on this Fourth Sunday in Ordinary Time.

Story source: "Perception," in William J. Bausch (Ed.), *A World of Stories for Preachers and Teachers,* Mystic, CT: Twenty-Third Publications, 1998, #69, pp. 214-215. Based on Steve Covey's *Seven Habits of Highly Effective People.*

Chapter 28

5th Sunday in Ordinary Time – C
Listening to God's Call

Scripture:

- Isaiah 6: 1-2a, 3-8
- Psalm 138: 1-2a, 2b-3, 4-5, 7c-8
- 1 Corinthians 15: 1-11
- Luke 5: 1-11

As we come together to celebrate the Eucharist on this Fifth Sunday in Ordinary Time, we hear, in all three readings, how God calls us to follow him.

In the first reading, God calls Isaiah to be his prophet. Isaiah at first argues that he is "unworthy" to be God's follower. However, after God assures him that this is not the case, Isaiah said, "Here I am, send me!" These words of Isaiah are the basis of one of the most popular hymns of our day, "Here I Am, Lord."

In the second reading, we hear how God called Paul. Though he started out as a great anti-Christian crusader, by following God's call and using God's grace he became one of the Church's greatest missionaries and writers.

And finally, in the Gospel, we hear how God called Simon Peter and two other fishermen, James and John, to become "fishers of men."

All of these stories are designed to teach us about God's call and our response. Sometimes, though, we just don't "get it." That is what the woman in the following story learned.

There once was a woman who thought she had a hearing problem. That is what her friends kept telling her when she constantly asked them to repeat what they had said.

So the woman made an appointment with a doctor who specialized in hearing problems. The doctor told the woman that he had lots of very fancy and expensive equipment to test her hearing, but he preferred using an old reliable test before using any of the expensive equipment. So, the doctor took out a common railroad pocket watch.

After seating himself across from the woman, the doctor held up the watch and asked her if she could hear it. "Yes, I hear it just fine," she replied. The doctor then got up and stood behind her and asked her again if she could hear it. Again she replied that she could. He then began increasing the distance from the woman, and each time he asked her if she could hear the ticking of the watch, she replied that she could hear it very well. Finally, the doctor went outside the room and asked her if she could hear the watch, and she replied that she could.

The doctor came back into the office and put the reliable old watch into his pocket. Looking at the woman, he gave her his diagnosis:

"Your hearing is perfect. Your problem is not with your hearing; your problem is that you don't listen."

From the Scripture stories and the story of the woman with a listening problem, here are three things we can learn.

First, everyone has a call from the Lord. In other words, everyone has a vocation. Often, though, we are not used to thinking in religious terms such as this. For example, for those of you who are married, what would you say if I asked you, "How did you know that God was calling you to the married state?" I imagine that you would have to do some serious thinking before you could answer. You probably didn't even think in those terms. Although we often talk about everyone having "a vocation," we need to always remember that God calls us to different things at different times of our lives.

Second, God talks to all of us. Sometimes, people are bewildered by the idea of God talking to them. Many times children have come to me after hearing that God talks to us. They tell me that at night, when they go to bed, they listen "really, really, really hard" but they just cannot hear God's voice. They think that they are supposed to hear an actual voice coming out of the sky talking to them.

That is not how God talks to us. Rather, God talks to us by way of our life experiences. God talks to us through our friends' conversations. God talks to us through the books we read, the television shows we watch, and the movies we see. God talks to us through religious leaders. God talks to us through the Scriptures. God talks to us through the mistakes we make and the victories we achieve. God talks to us via our desires and passions. God talks to us through our work and our leisure. The problem, though, is that often we do not listen. It's not that we are deliberately not listening to God, but rather, we often think that our experiences in the world are merely random, chaotic happenings.

To overcome a "listening problem," we need to retune our thinking. At the end of each day, for example, we could look over the day we have just experienced. We could reflect on the people we met, the conversations we heard, the things we read. We could then ask ourselves, "Why did God put these people in my life today? Why did God lead me to read this? How does this fit into the overall plan of my life?"

And third, God calls us to follow him not because we are worthy, but simply because it is our job to follow God. We act on this call out of obedience, not out of worthiness. Our calls are based on graces God gives us, not on how holy we are. There is a wonderful saying, "The will of God will never lead you to where the grace of God cannot keep you." In other words, to claim you are unworthy to be a follower of Christ is actually to say that the grace of God is insufficient or impotent. You really don't want to make such as statement, do you?

As we continue our life journeys this week, stop and listen. How is God speaking to you? How are you responding?

And that is the good news I have for you on this 5th Sunday in Ordinary Time.

Story source: Anonymous, "Hearing Problem," in Brian Cavanaugh (Ed.), *More Sower's Seeds: Second Planting,* New York: Paulist Press, 1992, #95, pp. 85-86.

Chapter 29

6th Sunday in Ordinary Time – C
Knock, Knock.

Scripture:

- Jeremiah 17: 5-8
- Psalm 1: 1-2, 3, 4 & 6
- 1 Corinthians 15: 12, 16-20
- Luke 6: 17, 20-26

On this Sixth Sunday in Ordinary Time, we have some very interesting Scripture selections. In the passages from Jeremiah and the psalmist, we learn that it is dangerous to place our trust in human beings. When we place our trust in them, we are like barren bushes in a harsh desert. But when we place our trust in the Lord, we flourish like a tree planted beside life-giving waters.

This theme is seen also in the Gospel passage that is sometimes called "the Sermon on the Plain." In this Gospel selection, Jesus reminds us that though we may be enjoying good times in this life, they may not last. Likewise, though, when we are having hard times in this life, they may not last either.

Taken all together, these Scriptures teach us to be humble, to place our trust in God and not to get caught up in worldliness. That is what is emphasized in the following ritual in Austria. I call this story, "Knock, knock. Who's there?"

There is a church in Vienna in which the members of the former royal family of Austria are buried. When royal funerals arrive at the church for burial rites, the people leading the funeral procession knock at the door to gain entrance.

On the other side of the door is the priest. Through the locked door, the priest asks, "Who is it that desires admission here?"

The funeral procession leader calls out, "His apostolic majesty, the emperor!"

The priest replies, "I don't know him."

The funeral procession leader knocks a second time. Once again, the priest asks, "Who is there?"

Again, the funeral procession leader replies, "the emperor."

The priest again replies that he does not know such a person.

Finally, a third knock is made. This time, after the priest asks who is there, the funeral procession leader answers, "A poor sinner, your brother." Only with this answer does the priest open the door to welcome the people who want to conduct the royal burial ceremony.

This is a wonderful story that reminds us whatever we experience on this earth will not last. Those who are having a wonderful life will lose it just as surely those who are having a hard life. In the end, we will all face eternity.

Most people, I think, can easily understand the Prophet Jeremiah and the psalmist when they say we will flourish when we place our trust in the Lord instead of human beings. It is a little bit more difficult, though, to make sense out of Jesus' "Sermon on the Plain."

Jesus says that the people who are "blessed" are those who are poor, hungry, hated, and weeping. On the other hand, he says woe to those who are rich and filled with food, who laugh and are praised by others. In the end, he promises that the tables will be turned.

But are poverty and hunger and sadness intrinsically good? Are having people hate you good? Is being rich and filled with food truly bad? Is laughter intrinsically bad? No. To understand this passage, we need the help of exegetes, experts in the Bible.

According to the exegetes, this passage was directed to followers and would-be followers of Jesus who led what we might call today "the good life." They had all that money could buy, and they were well respected by their society. In this sermon Jesus was not condemning them as a social class. Rather, he was challenging them. He was telling them not to be in love with the things of the world, things like money and power and prestige and good times. He told them to be thankful for what they had in this world, but always to be ready to share what they had with those who had less.

In this "Sermon on the Plain," Jesus was also telling those who had a hard time in this world that in the Kingdom of Heaven, things would be different. In other words, he was teaching about hope and trust in the Lord rather than in the world. That certainly must have been great news to those who had little in this life.

The message for us Christians of today is clear. We are to be thankful for what we have. We are to remember that every good gift comes from God. This includes such gifts as our energy, our health and the people who taught us our values. It includes the country we live in and the opportunities that we have which the overwhelming majority of the people of this world will never enjoy.

We need to avoid materialism, falling in love with the things of this life. We should own things, but never let things own us. And we should remember that every gift we have is to not only be developed and treasured, it is also to be shared with those in need.

When we can use our positions and gifts for the benefit of all our brothers and sisters, and are happy to do so, we have grasped the "Sermon on the Plain."

This week it would be a good idea to reflect on how we use our time, talent and treasure to help those in need.

And that is the good news I have for you on this Sixth Sunday in Ordinary Time.

Story source: "Death of a Hapsburg" in William J. Bausch (Ed.), *A World of Stories for Preachers and Teachers*, Mystic, CT: Twenty-Third Publications, 1998, #205, pp. 326-327.

Chapter 30

7th Sunday in Ordinary Time – C
I Had to Forgive

Scripture:

- 1 Samuel 26: 2, 7-9, 12-13, 22-23
- Psalm 103: 1-2, 3-4, 8 and 10, 12-13
- 1 Corinthians 15: 12, 45-49
- Luke 6: 27-38

Today, Catholic Christians celebrate the Seventh Sunday in Ordinary Time.

On this day, we hear some incredibly difficult and challenging commands that Jesus gives us. This homily focuses on the Christian commandment to forgive our enemies. Specifically, Jesus says, "To you who hear I say, love your enemies, do good to those who hate you, bless those who curse you, pray for those who mistreat you. To the person who strikes you on one cheek, offer the other one as well..." (Luke 6: 27-29). Jesus sums up the various teachings he has for us today by giving us what has come to be known as "The Golden Rule," that is, "Do to others as you would have them do to you" (Luke 6: 31).

Before discussing some important elements that we should know about Jesus' command to forgive our enemies, let's look at a story called, "I Had to Forgive My Enemy."

Mitchell was an 18-year old soldier in the United States Army at Fort Riley, Kansas in 1989. For the first year of his Army experience, he had a wonderful roommate. Then, in the second year, he got a roommate who he thought was the devil incarnate.

His new roommate, Thompson, hated the fact that Mitchell read the Bible and was trying to learn more about his Christian faith. In fact, the very first time Thompson walked into the room and saw Mitchell's Bible, he went into the hallway and shouted to the rest of the men in the outfit, "Hey, guys, we got a guy here with the Bible. You know what we have to do." Thompson then came back into the room and said, "When we finish with you, you will be just like us."

Thompson was a very lewd man in his speech and actions. He was a genuine bully, and he was big and strong. He loved to get into fights, and he often threatened younger soldiers with violence if they left their doors opened at night.

One day, Mitchell asked Thompson to come to church with him. Thompson became enraged and shouted, "Didn't I tell you I don't like church!" Immediately, Thompson picked up Mitchell by his ankles and slammed him into the wall four times. Although the great force of being slammed into the wall should have broken all of Mitchell's ribs, he remained unharmed. He felt the Lord had protected him. After Thompson let him go, all Mitchell did was laugh. This made Thompson surprised and confused. Thompson said, "I don't understand you. I just tried to hurt you, and all you can do is laugh?"

A couple months after this incident, however, Mitchell began to reflect on Thompson's violence and began to get angry. He began to think of getting even with Thompson.

Then, one day, Mitchell learned that Thompson had gotten frostbite on both of his feet and might have to have his feet amputated. Men of the unit began to tell Mitchell that Thompson wanted to see him very badly. Though Mitchell brushed off the suggestion that Thompson wanted to see him, he eventually did go to the hospital. Thompson told Mitchell that he had tremendous pain in both feet, and that even painkillers didn't work. He told Mitchell that surgeons might have to amputate both feet, and that he didn't want that. When Thompson showed Mitchell his feet, which were swollen and badly discolored, tears came to his eyes. All he could do was to pray with Thompson.

Three days later, Mitchell heard commotion downstairs. When he went to look, he say Thompson standing there, walking and taking baby steps. He thanked Mitchell for praying for him and said, "I knew God would hear your prayer." From then on, if anyone would try to give Mitchell grief for reading the Bible, Thompson would proclaim, "Leave Mitchell alone. Anybody that messes with Mitchell is going to have to fight me because he's praying for me!"

From Jesus' commandment for us to forgive and love our enemies, and from Mitchell's story, we can glean many things. Here are just three.

First, forgiveness means we give up resentment towards another person, and we cease wishing to "get even" for past harms. To forgive our enemies is a Christian commandment. We forgive because we are required to so as followers of Jesus Christ.

Second, forgiveness is an act of the will, not of emotions. To forgive another means we make a deliberate choice. Signs of our forgiveness include such things as: saying, "I forgive you;" ceasing to bad-mouth the other person; and not bringing up past hurtful incidents. Forgiving another does not mean we have to be friends with the other person, but as Christians, it does mean we need to love them, that is, to wish the best for them.

And third, to forgive others is good for our health – spiritual, mental, and physical. If we carry around resentments toward others, it only harms us, not them. Carrying around resentments is like having a cancer eating away our spirits. Resentments can lead to no good.

So as we continue our life journeys this week, it would be a good idea to reflect on our own lives. Is there anyone we need to forgive? If so, now is a great time to do it.

And that is the good news I have for you on this Seventh Sunday in Ordinary Time.

Story source: Anonymous, "I Had to Forgive My Enemy," www.experienceproject.com/ stories

Chapter 31

8th Sunday in Ordinary Time – C
Silence as Good Fruit

Scripture:

- Sirach 27: 4-7
- Psalm 92: 2-3, 13-14, 15-16
- 1 Corinthians 15: 54-59
- Luke 6: 39-45

Today, Catholic Christians celebrate the Eighth Sunday in Ordinary Time.

On this day, we hear about many concepts. This homily focuses on the wisdom we hear from the Book of Sirach. Specifically, we read: "When a sieve is shaken, the husks appear; so do one's faults when one speaks" (Sirach 27: 4). We then read, "The fruit of the tree shows the care it has had; so too does one's speech disclose the bent of one's mind. Praise no one before he speaks, for it is then that the people are tested" (Sirach 27: 6-7).

The phrase, "Praise no one before he speaks" is profound, for it is in speech that we can learn the character of a person. Obviously, we could approach this topic in a number of different ways. For today, though, we'll explore it in terms of the virtues of prudence and temperance and how those virtues often lead the wise person to silence.

Before exploring silence, however, let us look some modern examples of wise people putting prudence and temperance into action. The examples come from a newspaper advice columnist, Carolyn Hax, in her December column of December 28, 2015. In that day's column, Carolyn featured some letters from women who sang the praises of their mothers-in-law. Let's look at snippets from four women who wrote in to Carolyn.

Person #1 says:

"I adore my mother-in-law. She's great. We don't share a religion, which is very important to her, and she has never said a critical word to me in the 12 years I've been married to her son. She finds fun outings and focuses on making them toddler-friendly for our kids. She makes beautiful quilts and reads mystery novels. I try to make special time for her to spend with my husband without me and/or kids, and I like to spend time with her too."

Person #2 says, in part:

"My ex-mother-in-law told me just prior to my wedding that her mother-in-law had been petty and unpleasant, so she vowed to treat me like her own daughter. She did. She was kind and thoughtful and helpful without being intrusive. Even when her

son and I were divorcing, she never said an unkind word to me or about me."

Person #3 says, in part:

"When my then-new fiancé needed surgery, his mother told him her first instinct was to fly out to take care of him. Her second instinct was to stay home and let me fulfill my new role as his partner. She followed her second instinct – no hovering, no second-guessing."

And Person #4 says,

"My mother-in-law is fantastic, not because we always we always see eye-to-eye, but because she is able to NOT share everything she is thinking (dirty fridge, unfolded laundry, table not set). It is clear that she is driven nuts by these things, but oh, I am so appreciative of her rising above it and meeting us where we live."

From the reading from the Book of Sirach that we have today, and from the testimonies of the women who wrote into the advice columnist about their mothers-in-law, we can learn many things. Here are just three.

First, when we hear about the concept of the "fruit of a tree," the author is not speaking of results or consequences of our behavior. Rather, the "fruit of the tree" is our behavior itself. Oftentimes, people get this confused. They see a business prosper, for example, and believe that the success of the business is a sign that God is pleased with the owner. That is not necessarily the case. Often, saints live lives of extraordinary holiness, but their ministries do not show desired results.

Second, the author of Sirach is quite correct when he says we should not praise people before we hear them speak. This is because many people do not use the cardinal virtues of prudence and temperance before speaking. These virtues are associated with adulthood, for it usually only by making mistakes in speaking that we can learn to use these "filters" for our speech. Prudence refers to being cautious or using careful good judgment, while temperance refers to using moderation of voluntary self-restraint. In the each of the mother-in-law stories, we see temperance and prudence in speech abundantly present, and the mothers-in-law showed these virtues by silence.

And third, thoughts and silence are not behaviors. Many Catholic Christians fail to distinguish between the two things. Bad behaviors related to speech include gossip, slander, vulgar or lewd language, harmful words, self-important bragging, lying, know-it-all talk, and others. Prudent and temperate persons, even if they harbor inclinations to use such language in their heads, refrain from doing so. What comes out of their mouths is pure. They are showing good "fruit."

As we continue our life journeys this week, it would be a good idea to reflect on what comes out of our mouths. Do we use profane, vulgar, or obscene language? Do we deliberately use language that hurts others? Do we lie to make ourselves seem important to others? Are we braggarts? Is what comes out of our mouths worthy of being the same mouth that receives Holy Communion when we come to Eucharist?

And that is the good news I have for you on this Eighth Sunday in Ordinary Time.

Story source: Carolyn Hax, "Readers Celebrate Their Mothers-In-Law," *Tell Me about It* column, December 28, 2015.

Chapter 32

9th Sunday in Ordinary Time – C
The Blue Book

Scripture:

- 1 Kings 8: 41-43
- Psalm 117: 1, 2
- Galatians 1: 1-2, 6-10
- Luke 7: 1-10

Today, Catholic Christians celebrate the Ninth Sunday in Ordinary Time.

On this day, we encounter a beautiful story of faith in the Gospel of Luke. In this story, a centurion sent word to Jesus that his slave was ill. He had faith that Jesus could cure his slave.

Many of the Jews knew about the centurion and urged Jesus to come to the centurion's house. They told Jesus that this particular centurion loved the nation of Israel and had even built a synagogue for them.

As a result of the people's good words, Jesus headed out to the centurion's house to cure the slave. We read, "And Jesus went with them, but when he was only a short distance from the house, the centurion sent friends to tell him, 'Lord, do not trouble yourself, for I am not worthy to have you enter under my roof. Therefore, I did not consider myself worthy to come to you; but say the word and let my servant be healed'" (Luke 7: 6-7).

Jesus was amazed at the faith of the centurion. In fact, he said to the crowds who were following him, "I tell you, not even in Israel have I found such faith" (Luke 7: 9). When the centurion's messengers returned to their master's house, they discovered that the slave had been cured.

Catholic Christians are very familiar with the phrase, "Lord, I am not worthy," for we say it at every Eucharist before receiving Holy Communion.

Before looking more closely at the idea of our unworthiness before the Lord, however, let's look at an amusing story by author Jeff Bordon called, "Do You Know Me?"

There was once a history professor in a large university who was giving a final exam to the 250 students in his freshman class. Because it was such a large lecture course, there was no way he could possibly know the names of all the students.

In this essay exam, students had to write their answers in standard college "blue books." When the two-hour time limit was up, the professor announced that the test was over and that the students should place their booklets in a pile on his desk.

The professor sat back in his chair and watched as the 250 students in the auditorium filed past his desk, dropped their booklets off, and exited the room.

As the professor prepared to sort through the pile of tests on his desk, he noticed that one young man was still in his seat, writing answers.

The professor cleared his throat loudly, but the student didn't seem to notice. The professor called to the student, "Young man, the test is over! Come down here now and hand in your blue book!"

The student didn't even look up.

The professor decided to teach the young man a lesson. He sat back down at his desk and waited. The professor decided that when the student came up to turn in his test, he would take the student's booklet, rip it to shreds, and give him an "F" for the semester.

Five minutes went by. Then ten. Finally, after twenty minutes, the student closed his test booklet and made his way down to the now-fuming professor.

"I'm finished," the student said.

The professor answered incredulously, "Do you think I'm going to accept your exam now?"

The young man leaned forward, looking over the stack of identical-looking blue books on the desk. His eyes narrowed and he frowned just slightly.

The young man then asked, "Do you have any idea who you're talking to?"

The professor angrily replied, "I don't know, and I don't care!"

"Good," replied the student. And with that, the student stuck his test booklet right in the middle of the stack of other booklets and walked out of the room.

Though we can sometimes fool professors, we can't fool God. God can see all, and that is what we learn in the healing of the centurion's slave story. Here are three things we need to keep in mind.

First, God calls each one of us to do something with our life. Not only are we called to follow a vocation path in terms of an occupation, we are also called to follow Jesus as Christians.

Second, none of us are "worthy" of our call to follow Christ. Our lives and our calls are pure gifts from God. What we do with our calls are our gifts to God.

And third, just because we see ourselves as "unworthy," that is no reason for us to not follow God's call. If you ever visited a Catholic seminary, you would most likely be amazed at the collection of men you'd find. If you are anything like me, you would think, "I can't believe God would call some of these men to be priests! I could think of hundreds of others who would be much better choices!" But, God's ways are not our ways, and God's thoughts are not our thoughts.

As we continue our life journeys this week, it would be a good idea to reflect on our own calls from God. How are we striving to do the best we can with the gifts God gave us?

And that is the good news I have for you on this Ninth Sunday in Ordinary Time.

Story source: Jeff Bordon, "Do You Know Me?," in Wayne Rice (Ed.), *Hot Illustrations for Youth Talks 4*, Grand Rapids, MI: Youth Specialties/Zondervan, 2001, pp. 68-69.

Chapter 33

10th Sunday in Ordinary Time – C
St. Olga

Scripture:

- 1 Kings 17: 17-24
- Psalm 30: 2 & 4, 5-6, 11 & 12a & 13b
- Galatians 1: 11-19
- Luke 7: 11-17

Today, Catholic Christians celebrate the Tenth Sunday in Ordinary Time.

On this day, we hear about how St. Paul went from being a persecutor of the Church to a great apostle to the gentiles, that is, to non-Jewish persons. Paul, in his Letter to the Galatians, says, "For you heard of my former way of life in Judaism, how I persecuted the church of God beyond measure and tried to destroy it, and progressed in Judaism beyond many of my contemporaries among my race, since I was even more a zealot for my ancestral traditions. But when God, who from my mother's womb had set me apart and called me through his grace, was pleased to reveal his Son to me, so that I might proclaim him to the Gentiles, my immediate response was not to consult any human being" (Galatians 1: 13-16).

Hearing such conversion stories is always inspiring, for it reminds us that there is always hope for us. It is never too late to get off the path of darkness, and turn, instead, to the path of light. That is what we see in the life of St. Olga, one of the most bloodthirsty women in the history of the Church.

Olga, often called Helga, was born around 890 and was a member of the Norse people who had invaded lands along the Volga River. Although the accounts of her life are somewhat sketchy, they all point to an incredible ruthlessness toward her enemies.

When she grew up, she married Igor of Kiev, who was the ruler of the Russian kingdom. Together, they produced a son, Prince Svyatoslav. The entire family was pagan.

When Svyatoslav was only three-years old, a people known as the Drevlians killed Igor, thus making Olga the ruler of the land.

The death of her husband enraged Olga, and she vowed to get revenge. With Igor out of the way, the Drevlians came up with a plan to have Olga marry their prince, Mal. This would make Mal the ruler of that part of Russia. Olga, however, was not willing to give up her power, for she wanted to preserve it for her son.

To present their plans to Olga, the Drevlians sent twenty of their best men to persuade Olga to marry Mal. When they arrived, she burned them alive. She then sent word to Prince Mal that she had accepted the proposal for marriage, but that she wanted him to send his best men to accept the offer of marriage. When the men arrived, she gave them a warm welcome and an invitation to clean up after a long journey. Once the men were in the bathhouse, she locked the doors and set the building on fire, killing them all.

With Mal's best men out of the way, she invited the remaining Drevlians to a funeral feast for her husband. After the Drevlians were drunk, Olga's soldiers killed over 5,000 of them. Olga tried to burn the surviving Drevlians to death, but some of them escaped, some were killed, and some were made slaves.

Around 957, Olga became a Christian by being baptized in Constantinople. She persuaded Emperor Otto I of that empire to send missionaries to Kiev. He sent St. Adalbert of Magdeburg there. Unfortunately, Christianity did not catch on too quickly, and her son, Svyatoslav, never did become a Christian. Her grandson, St. Vladimir, did bring the faith to the land.

When her son was old enough to rule, Olga retired from public life but continued her missionary efforts, and she had many churches built. St. Olga's feast day is July 11.

Now when we look at how people such as Olga and Paul went from a life of grave evil to a life of goodness, we have to be amazed. I doubt that any of us has a history that can begin to match that of Olga. Such stories are good to hear, though, for it gives all of us hope, for if characters such as Olga and Paul can repent, so can we.

From examining their lives, and from the Scripture of today, we can learn many things. Here are just three.

First, very few of us are "natural" saints. Rather, most of us are what I call "garden variety" sinners – people who commit what most would call "common, everyday" sins. Certainly there are many exceptions, people who seemed to be saintly from the very earliest ages, such as St. Therese, the Little Flower. Most of us, though, don't fit that category.

Second, God's grace enables all people to change their way of life, moving from darkness to light. All we have to do is look through the long history of the Catholic Church and read the lives of the saints to know this. That is wonderful news for all of us who sometimes wonder if we will ever stop doing wrong. One of the greatest things we can gain from reading the lives of the saints, especially those who went from "very bad" to "very good" living, is hope for ourselves, and faith in the power of God's grace in our lives.

And third, we should never judge others too harshly, for we don't know the end of the story of anyone's life. Certainly if we had judged Paul when he was the terrorist known as Saul, or if we had judged Olga when she was busy burning people to death, we would have missed the good part of their stories – the conversion part. And it is the conversion part of people's stories that is the romantic, happily-ever-after part of the story that the Catholic worldview espouses.

As we continue our life journeys this week, it would be a good idea to reflect on our own lives. What kind of conversion story are we weaving with God's grace?

And that is the good news I have for you on this Tenth Sunday in Ordinary Time.

Story sources:

"St. Olga," in *Butler's Lives of the Saints: New Full Edition,* revised by Peter Doyle, Collegeville, Minnesota: Burns & Oates, The Liturgical Press, 1999, pp. 82-83.

"St. Olga of Kiev," *Wikipedia.*

Chapter 34

11th Sunday in Ordinary Time - C
Lincoln Forgives

Scripture:

- 2 Samuel 12: 7-10, 13
- Psalm 32: 1-2, 5, 7, 11
- Galatians 2: 16, 19-21
- Luke 7: 36 - 8: 3

As we come to celebrate the Eleventh Sunday in Ordinary Time, we read the fascinating story of "the woman with the alabaster box" washing Jesus' feet with her tears and drying them with her long hair.

In this story, we see that this woman was very unpopular with the other people attending. In fact, they judged her to be beneath them; they considered themselves to be morally superior to her. Jesus, on the other hand, saw what the other guests did not see. He was able to see her heart and soul, to see the goodness that totally escaped the notice of those who were judging her so harshly.

Like Jesus, we too are called to search for the goodness that lies in each person. We too are called to forgive the failings of others, just as we ask God to forgive us. Some people are able to do this more easily than others. Such was the case of President Abraham Lincoln, the Sixteenth President of the United States and one of the most greatly admired of all Presidents.

When Mr. Lincoln was running for the presidency, there was a man who absolutely hated him. That man's name was Edwin McMasters Stanton. Stanton used all his energy saying bad things about Lincoln in public. He even made fun of Lincoln's physical appearance and tried to embarrass him at every point in the campaign.

Now one of the first tasks a new President has is to select a cabinet, people who will head important agencies of the federal government and help him implement his programs. Lincoln went about this task, selecting the best men for the job. (In those days, it was unthinkable that an American president would choose a woman for such a job.)

After picking many men for cabinet positions, the day came for President Lincoln to choose a person for the all-important post of Secretary of War. He calmly chose Edwin Stanton, the man who had been such a thorn in his side throughout the campaign. The people who supported Lincoln were horrified. They told the President that he was making a big mistake in choosing Stanton. They said, "Mr. President, don't you know Stanton and all the bad things he has said about you? He is your enemy. He will sabotage your programs."

Mr. Lincoln's reply was short and to the point: "Yes, I know Mr. Stanton. I am aware of all the terrible things he has said about me. But after looking over the nation, I find he is the best man for the job." So Edwin Stanton became Lincoln's Secretary of War, and did an excellent job serving his nation and his President.

Not many years later, President Lincoln was assassinated. Many wonderful things were said about him, but Stanton's words were the most powerful. Standing near the body of the man he had once hated, he said Mr. Lincoln was one of the greatest men who ever lived. Mr. Stanton said of Lincoln, "He now belongs to the ages."

Now if President Lincoln had hated Stanton, both men would have gone to their graves as enemies. But through the power of love and forgiveness, Mr. Lincoln transformed an enemy into a friend.

Because we, too, are called to imitate Jesus Christ in our lives, we must always search for the good in others. We must forgive for the greater good. That means that we forgive not only to avoid having our souls and mind eaten up with the spiritual cancer of hate, but to build the Kingdom of God on Earth.

Examples of how this works are all around us. In the workplace, for example, good leaders seek to serve the needs of the whole organization. As a result, they search for people who can "make things happen."

Oftentimes the people they choose are not what we would call saintly people. The leader did not choose them for their saintliness. Rather, she or he chose them for their clarity of thought, their organizational ability, their skill, and their ability to accomplish goals. This happens in all organizations whether we are talking about a huge retailer like Wal-Mart or Target, a car manufacturer like Ford or Toyota, or a religious organization like a Catholic diocese.

Good leaders are able to forgive the failings of people they need to make things happen. But we are called to forgive the failings of others not just to further an organization's needs or to make ourselves free from the spiritual cancer of hate. We are called to stop judging others and to begin forgiving others because our Lord and Savior, Jesus Christ, commanded us to do this. This is a Christian commandment. This is not merely a Christian "suggestion."

Now I know, just as you know, it is very hard to discern the good in some people. There are some people whom we dislike so intensely that our feelings about them cloud our ability to find the good in them.

Nevertheless, they are God's children, our brothers and sisters. And are we not to give our family members the benefit of the doubt? Of course we are.

As we continue our life journeys this week, it would be a good idea to ask ourselves how we judge others harshly and how we fail to forgive their failings.

And that is the good news I have for you on this Eleventh Sunday in Ordinary Time.

Story source: Anonymous, "Loving Your Enemies," in Brian Cavanaugh (Ed.), *The Sower's Seeds*, New York: Paulist Press, 1990, #91, pp. 72-74.

Chapter 35

12th Sunday in Ordinary Time – C
The Kebbitch Itch

Scripture:

- Zechariah 12: 10-11; 13:1
- Psalm 63: 2, 3-4, 5-6, 8-9
- Galatians 3: 26-29
- Luke 9: 18-24

As we come together to celebrate the Eucharist on this Twelfth Sunday in Ordinary Time, we hear Jesus telling us that we are to take up our cross each day and follow in his footsteps. The "crosses" that Jesus is referring to are the problems we face each day.

This seems like a simple command, but strangely enough, all of us fail at times to take up our crosses each day in a mature manner. This is exactly what happened in the following old Hassidic Jewish story told by author Wayne Rice.

There was once a woman named Anna Kebbitch who was known by all as a complainer. In fact, many people even called her "Anna the Complainer." Anna complained that she had too little money and that her clothes were rags. She complained about her bad back and the fact that she had to walk to draw water for her house. She complained that her house was too small and that her children hardly ever visited her.

One day, Anna Kebbitch woke up with an itch on her nose. Even scratching her nose did not stop the itch. Therefore, Anna went into town to visit the rabbi.

When the rabbi saw Anna, he asked, "How are you, Anna?"

Anna replied, "I am so poor that my clothes are like rags. My health is so bad that my back feels like the walls of Jericho. I have to walk so far to draw water for my house that my feet are like watermelons. My house is so small I can hardly move around in it. My children visit so seldom that they hardly know me anymore. And now, on top of all my problems, I have a terrible itch on my nose that simply won't go away. Tell, me, Rabbi, what does this mean?"

The rabbi replied, "Anna, your itch is the Kebbitch itch—the 'complainer's itch.' It simply means this: However you consider yourself, so shall you be."

Well, the next morning Anna's nose was still itching. In fact, the itch was worse than ever. Her back really did feel as if it had turned to stone like the walls of Jericho. When she looked around her house, she noticed that the house had shrunk so much that her arms stuck out of the windows and her legs hung out the front door. She could not even turn around in it. On the ends of her legs were two gigantic watermelons, and her clothes had turned into rags. When her son and daughter came walking by, Anna called out to them but they kept on walking by, ignoring her. And her nose itched worse than ever.

In despair, Anna thought carefully about what the Rabbi had told her: *However you consider yourself, so shall you be.*

So, Anna began to think to herself, "Actually, I have enough money to live on and a little left over. From now on, I will help those who are much poorer than me with my abundance. And my health really is not so bad. In fact, for someone my age, I feel quite well. As for my house, it is not large, but it is a nice little house, comfortable and warm. I don't really mind walking to draw water because I can stop and smell the flowers along the way there. And as for my children, I am proud of them. They are independent and can take care of themselves."

As soon as Anna said these things to herself, her nose stopped itching, and her life returned to normal. Anna's outlook on life brightened considerably, and she kept her bright outlook forever. Today, when rabbis tell this story, they always end with this statement: "May your noses itch forever."

All of us, from time to time, grumble about our lives. We focus on the negative things and not on the positives. We fail to carry our crosses gracefully.

Jesus, however, asks us to carry our daily crosses. First, however, we need to identify them. Our cross might be a problematic child, a bad marriage, a spouse with an alcohol problem, a job that we don't like, credit card debt, an addiction to alcohol or cigarettes, overeating, procrastination, or something else.

Second, we need to distinguish between those crosses we can change and those we cannot. For example, we can pay off our debt or forgive a friend who has hurt us, but we cannot change the personality of the mother-in-law who is always criticizing us.

Third, we can take steps to prevent further problems or daily crosses. For example, people who have problems with impulse spending should not be wandering around malls with money or credit cards in their pockets.

Fourth, for those life problems that we can change, we should take steps to do so. It is no good to complain that we have a job that doesn't pay enough or that we have a job that we don't like. Go back to school. Prepare for something that pays more and that you like better. Complaining will not get you a raise, nor will it get you a job you like. It will just make others not want to be around you!

Fifth, when we are faced with problems that we have no control over, turn them over to God. He will be happy to help you carry those crosses.

Finally, give thanks to God every day for the blessings he has given you. By the time you finish giving thanks, you will be amazed to learn that your problems are probably not as great as you thought.

And that's the good news I have for you on this Twelfth Sunday in Ordinary Time.

Story source: Anonymous, "The Kebbitch Itch," in Wayne Rice (Ed.), *Hot Illustrations for Youth Talks,* Grand Rapids, MI: Youth Specialties/Zondervan, 1993, p. 128-130.

Chapter 36

13th Sunday in Ordinary Time – C
The Grain of Rice

Scripture:

- 1 Kings 19: 16b, 19-21
- Psalm 16: 1-2a & 5, 7-8, 9-10, 11
- Galatians 5: 1, 13-18
- Luke 9: 51-62

As we come together to celebrate the Thirteenth Sunday in Ordinary Time, we are challenged to put our faith into action. In Paul's letter to the Galatians, for example, we hear that the whole law is filled in one commandment that has two parts: "You shall love your neighbor as yourself" (Galatians 5: 14). And in the Gospel, Jesus tells us to keep our mind on building the kingdom, to not look back. Once we realize we are followers of Christ, we are to move ever forward.

As Catholic Christians, we realize that our strength comes from Jesus' gift of the Eucharist. In fact, we call the Eucharist or Mass the "source and summit" of our spirituality. But we celebrate Mass and receive Holy Communion not as something separate from the rest of our lives. On the contrary, we are supposed to take the graces we receive from Mass and Communion and put them into action in our daily lives. Putting gifts into action is what one young lady learned very well in the following story.

There was once a king with four daughters. One day he decided he needed to get away for a few years to pray. In his absence, he left his four daughters in charge of running the kingdom.

Though they were frightened to have all this responsibility, the king was determined to go to a distant monastery. Before he left, however, he gave each of them a gift of a single grain of rice. He told them that he prayed that his gifts would help them learn how to rule wisely. With that, he left.

The first daughter, the eldest, wrapped her grain with a golden thread and put it inside a beautiful crystal box and looked at it every day.

The second daughter put her grain of rice inside a wooden box and put it under her bed and forgot about it.

The third daughter, the most practical of the three, looked at the grain of rice and said to herself, "This is like any other grain of rice" and promptly threw it away.

The fourth daughter, who was the youngest, wondered about the significance of the gift. She kept the gift for a whole year before she understood its meaning.

After some years, the king returned to the kingdom. After greeting his daughters, he got the report from each one as to what she had done with the gift he had given her.

The first daughter brought her grain of rice wrapped with the thread of gold, and the second daughter brought hers from under the bed in its wooden box. The king said, "Thank you." The third daughter ran into the kitchen, took a grain of rice from the rice jar, and gave it to the king. He also thanked her.

When it came to the fourth daughter, though, she told her father, the king, that she had planted it in the ground. Soon it grew and spread. From the rice, she gathered seeds and planted those. This she did every year. "Come outside, Father, and see what the grain of rice has produced." The king was incredibly pleased to see beautiful crops of rice as far as the eye could see. There was now enough rice to feed the entire nation.

The king then took off his crown and put it on the fourth daughter's head, saying, "You have learned the meaning of how to rule." From that day on, the youngest daughter ruled many years, wisely and well.

In this story, the King is like Jesus, and the daughters are his followers. The first three daughters did not live up to their calling, for they failed to nourish the gift that the father had given them. The fourth daughter, though, took her gift and multiplied it. She was pro-active.

That is exactly what we are to do with the gifts God has given us. In the passage from Galatians that we have today, for example, we are told we must put ourselves in each other's service. That means to go outside of self and become other-directed. We must deliberately search for Christ who lives in each of us and put our Faith into action.

Many Christians, unfortunately, don't do that. They think that to be a good Christian all they have to do is avoid public wrongdoing. For example, they don't rob banks or shoot people. As a result, they walk around proud as peacocks, thinking they are holier than others. They might cheat on their tax forms, and they might harm others by their gossipy tongues, but because they do not end up in prison for such things, they see themselves as morally superior to others. They don't have a clue as to what it means to be a follower of Christ.

And in today's Gospel, Jesus commands us to follow him. To follow him means that we are to be pro-active. We are to engage in the spiritual works of mercy such as consoling the sorrowful and the corporal works of mercy such as sheltering the homeless or visiting the sick or imprisoned.

Each one of us here today has been given different gifts from God, and every one of us is to be like the fourth daughter in the story. We are not to glorify or bury our gifts like the first two daughters, or discard them like the third. On the contrary, we are to respect, develop, multiply, and share our gifts with Christ who lives in our brothers and sisters.

And that is the good news I have for you on this Thirteenth Sunday in Ordinary Time.

Story source: Anonymous, "The Grain of Rice," in Brian Cavanaugh (Ed.), *Sower's Seeds of Encouragement: 5th Planting,* 1998, #49, pp. 42-43.

Chapter 37

14ᵗʰ Sunday in Ordinary Time – C
Dr. Susan Nagele

Scripture:

- Isaiah 66: 10-14c
- Psalm 66: 1-3a, 4-5, 6-7a, 16 & 20
- Galatians 6: 14-18
- Luke 10: 1-12, 17-20

Every Fourth of July, Americans celebrate Independence Day, the birthday of a new nation they called the United States of America. Part of the celebration is to look back over the history of our nation and focus attention on the things we have done well as a country. One of the great things American Catholic Christians may be especially proud of is the sending of American Catholic missionaries throughout the world. And that is a wonderful fact to ponder as we read the Gospel passage for this Fourteenth Sunday in Ordinary Time.

In this Gospel, we hear Jesus commissioning seventy-two people to take the Good News to all corners of the Earth. This mandate is just as relevant today as it was two thousand years ago.

In the early days of the United States, missionaries from Europe brought the Catholic faith to our country. Especially influential were missionaries from Spain and Ireland.

But mission territories are expected to "grow up," to become independent, to pull their own weight on the world stage. And that is what two men accomplished in the early 1900s. Fr. Thomas Frederick "Freddy" Price of Wilmington, N.C., and Bishop James Anthony Walsh of Boston, founded the Catholic Foreign Mission Society of America. This organization, more commonly called Maryknoll, was established to send American priests and Brothers to foreign lands to spread Catholic Christianity. Later, the Maryknoll Sisters institute was founded, and after the Second Vatican Council, a third part of Maryknoll was founded, the lay missionaries.

Like the priests, Brothers, and Sisters who went before them, the lay missionaries went abroad to spread the Good News of Jesus Christ by using their many talents. One such person was Susan Nagele.

The seeds to the lay missionary vocation seem to have been sown early in life for Susan when she visited her uncle, Fr. Joe, who was a Glenmary Missionary priest in Appalachia. Susan got to see poverty first hand. The Glenmary Missionaries work in poor areas of rural America.

In college, Susan was influenced not only by contact with the Catholic Newman Center at the University of Illinois, but also by short mission trips she took to Nicaragua and the Dominican Republic.

Through these experiences, God touched Susan's heart and firmly planted what some call the "Missionary Spirit." Though she treasured the little mission trips, her heart longed for more.

After graduating from the Southern Illinois University Medical School, Susan immediately joined the Maryknoll Lay Missionaries. She knew she did not want to become a Maryknoll Sister, but she did want to devote a nice chunk of time to the missions.

After studying at Maryknoll, New York, Dr. Nagele spent her first six years as a missionary with Maryknoll in Tanzania. Later, she spent six years in southern Sudan, the only physician to serve two refugee camps with a combined population of more than thirty thousand people. Susan also worked in Kenya.

Today Maryknoll continues to be the biggest source of Catholic missionaries from the United States to the rest of the world. Today Maryknoll priests, Brothers, Sisters, and Lay Missionaries serve in nations of Asia, Africa, South America, Central America, and in Mexico.

Most American Catholics will not follow in Susan Nagele's footsteps by leaving the United States for foreign countries. Nevertheless, the call to missions is something all Catholic Christians have by virtue of their baptism. So if we do have this call, and we do not plan to go to foreign lands to spread the Good News as Maryknoll Lay Missionary Susan Nagele did, how do we meet our missionary obligations?

First, we can pray for the Catholic men and women who serve on the front lines in mission territories, giving their lives for their faith. That is exactly what St. Therese, the "Little Flower," did in her Carmelite convent in France. In fact, so great was her prayer life for foreign missionaries, that the Church has declared her to be one of the patron saints of foreign missions, along with St. Francis Xavier.

Second, we can support foreign missions financially. Many missionaries serve in nations that are desperately poor. They have no hope of getting financial help for supplies except from Americans who are blessed with so much.

Finally, we can help meet our missionary mandate by encouraging and supporting fellow parishioners who take mission trips to foreign lands. Such trips can have a profound effect on people's lives, as we see in the life of Susan Nagele. God used the one-and two-week mission trips she took in college to plant the "missionary spirit" seed in her heart.

As we continue our life journey this week, it might be a good idea to ask ourselves how we meet our call to mission that we received in Baptism.

And that is the good news I have for you on the Fourteenth Sunday in Ordinary Time.

Story source: Tom Roberts, "The Emerging Church: To Be Part of the Everyday World," *National Catholic Reporter,* Vol. 46, No. 18, pp. 1, 16-17.

Chapter 38

15th Sunday in Ordinary Time – C
Neighbors & Sam Rayburn

Scripture:

- Deuteronomy 30: 10-14
- Psalm 69: 14 & 17, 30-31, 33-34, 36ab & 37
- Colossians 1: 15-20
- Luke 10: 25-37

On this Fifteenth Sunday in Ordinary Time, we hear Jesus' story that has become known as "The Good Samaritan" story. This is one of the "good guy-bad guy" types of stories that Jesus liked to tell.

In the story, a man is beaten up, robbed, and left to die on the side of the road. Two highly respected members of the Jewish community, a priest and a Levite, ignored the battered man. A Samaritan, though, took pity on him. Not only did he care for him, he brought him to an inn and paid for the man to be taken care of for some days. The Samaritan showed love, while the priest and Levite showed no love, no compassion.

This story must have made Jesus' Jewish listeners very uncomfortable, for the people who they considered to be the "good guys" of their society were the "bad guys" of the story, while the Samaritan was the "good guy." And as you know, the Jews hated the Samaritans.

But what does all this have to do with us today? Plenty. We are called by Jesus to be people of love, and we are called to put this love into action. That is what the triple love command of Jesus is all about—not only to love God, neighbor, and self, but also to show this love in how we live.

One man who gave us an excellent example of how to put this love into action was a Texan who served for many years as the Speaker of the United States' House of Representatives. His name was Sam Rayburn.

One day, Sam learned that the daughter of one of his friends had been critically injured in a car accident. The next morning, Sam went to his friend's house to see if he could be of help.

The father of the injured daughter said that there was nothing that could be done.

Sam replied, "Well, have you had your morning coffee yet?"

The father replied that he and his family had not taken the time to make coffee or have their breakfast. So, Sam began preparing fresh coffee and making breakfast. While he was busy doing that, the father came into the kitchen and said, "Mr. Speaker, I thought you were supposed to be having breakfast at the White House this morning."

Sam replied, "I was, but I called the President and told him I had a friend who was in need and that I couldn't come to the White House."

Sam Rayburn's action was a brilliant example of love of neighbor. From this story, and the story of the Good Samaritan, we can learn three things.

First, we need to define what "love" is. If you look in a dictionary, you will see that "love" has many different meanings. For love of neighbor, which is the highlight of Jesus' story today, love may be defined as wishing the best for another person. I have never found a better definition of love of neighbor.

Wishing the best for another person is not an emotion. Rather, it is an act of the will. This means that it does not matter if we like another person or not. As a child of God, every human being is worthy of respect and dignity. Wishing the best for another is something we can will without actually liking the person.

In my role as a priest, I find myself helping many people who are in need. Many of them I have never met and have absolutely no preconceived notions about them. That they are human and in need are all I need to know. Others, perhaps, may be difficult people filled with hatred, rage, self-righteousness, or bigotry. I help them, also, if they are in need of anointing, counseling, food, shelter, a sounding board to vent, or whatever. Though such people are not as enjoyable to help as others, it is a moral mandate from Jesus to do so. To show one's love is not to depend on our emotionally "liking" or "disliking" another person. It is to be based on Christ's commandment to us as His followers.

Second, love is the highest virtue, taking precedence over all others. As a teenager, for example, I was in what was called in those days a "junior seminary." It was for high school youth who thought they wanted to become priests.

Part of the rules called for silence during certain hours or in certain places on the campus. However, the priests who ran the seminary taught us "charity trumps all else." Therefore, if a fellow student was in need, it was not only permissible to break the silence and help him, it was a moral obligation.

Third, we need to realize who our "neighbor" is. Like the word "love," the word "neighbor" has many different meanings. Frequently in our language it means a person who lives in the same part of town we live in. In Jesus' stories, however, a "neighbor" is anyone in need.

Much more than in Jesus' time, we are able to see all kinds of people in need. We see people suffering from earthquakes in Haiti, hurricanes in New Orleans, famines in Ethiopia, tsunamis in Indonesia, and the like.

Because of this, we must realize that all of humanity is our neighbor. Therefore, as Christian people, we put our love into action when the need arises.

And that is the good news I have for you on this Fifteenth Sunday in Ordinary Time.

Story source: Anonymous, "Make a Difference," in Brian Cavanaugh (Ed.), *Fresh Sower's Seeds: Third Planting,* New York: Paulist Press, 1994, #64, p. 61.

Chapter 39

16th Sunday in Ordinary Time - C
Mary, Martha, and the Jungle

Scripture:

- Genesis 18: 1-10a
- Psalm 15: 2-3a, 3bc-4ab, 5
- Colossians 1: 24-28
- Luke 10: 38-42

As we come together to celebrate the Eucharist on this Sixteenth Sunday in Ordinary Time, we hear the fascinating story of Mary and Martha, two sisters who were friends of Jesus. In this story, we see Martha working very hard to put a meal on the table for dinner, while Mary sits and chats with Jesus. Martha is rather upset with her sister for not helping her get dinner ready, but Jesus tells her to relax.

For centuries, scholars and spiritual writers have tried to make sense out of this story. Some have taken Martha's side, while others have taken Mary's side. Unfortunately, in their quest for understanding, many of these people have polarized this beautiful and simple story. Human beings often polarize things they do not understand. That is exactly what author Fred Spencer discovered when he encountered a jungle.

Now if you are like me, you have never been in a genuine jungle. And, if you're like me, you probably have some preconceived notions about what jungles must be like, perhaps from Tarzan movies or adventure channels on television.

One man who has been in a jungle was F. Spencer Chapman, author of a book named *The Jungle Is Neutral.* Chapman was a British army officer during World War Two, stationed on the island colony of Singapore, off the tip of the Malay Peninsula. The British army believed that no invasion could ever get through the jungle to their north, so any attack on Singapore would have to come from the sea.

To their amazement, however, the Japanese did come from the north through the thick jungles of the peninsula to attack the garrison that Chapman was part of. Singapore fell very quickly.

Fortunately, Chapman escaped into the jungle, and he spent nine months living there before he was able to rejoin his fellow soldiers.

Chapman had heard two conflicting reports about the jungle. Therefore, at the time of his escape into the jungle, he did not have a clear idea of what to expect. On the one hand, he had heard that jungles were fearsome places filled with snakes and insects, poisonous fruit, and wild animals. Therefore, anyone who ever got lost in a jungle would surely die.

On the other hand, Chapman had heard that jungles were like lush, tropical paradises, filled with fresh water and wonderful fruits. In other words, it was a place where just about anyone could survive with relative ease.

The truth that Chapman discovered in his nine months in the jungle is that jungles are neutral. They are neither inherently destructive to people by making it impossible to survive, nor are they naturally supportive of people. Rather, survival depends on the individual. The more effort that the person puts into survival, the greater the chances the person will survive. Chapman was able to make of the jungle what he wished it to be.

Many people approach the world that God gave us as a jungle. Some see the world mostly as a negative place, a place filled with evil just waiting to harm them. In their heads, sin is the usual course of human events, while grace is something rare and limited to highly favored persons such as themselves. Because of their view of the world, they often carry around anger and fear and suspicion in their hearts. This is a common fundamentalist view.

Other people, though, see the world and its people as intrinsically good, for God created them. In their view, sin is an abnormal happening, something that goes against the usual course of events. These are the people who are able to find joy everywhere and, not surprisingly, find their hearts filled with gratitude. This is the true Catholic view.

So what *is* the world like? Is it basically good or basically evil?

These questions are natural ones for people to ask, for people have always tended to view reality in poles: good and evil, right and wrong, work life and home life; light and dark, night and day, yin and yang, success and failure, and the like.

Thus, it is not surprising that over the centuries many people have tried to find polarization in the story of Mary and Martha.

Many have said the story this means the contemplative life, symbolized by Mary's talking to Jesus, is superior to the missionary life, symbolized by Martha's hard work of service. Others have thought that the story means that prayer is more important than action. Such views are both arrogant and ignorant. All vocations are precious in the eyes of God, and the superior vocation is the one that God asks each individual to follow. We need both. We need balance.

I think a good way to view the story is to see prayer as the fuel that we need to carry out our mandate as Christians to be lights to the world. We cannot feed the hungry, console the sorrowful, or live out our vocations without the power of prayer.

Thus, instead of polarizing this story, perhaps we should agree that we need to be both Mary and Martha, combining prayer and action.

And that is the good news I have for you on this Sixteenth Sunday in Ordinary Time.

Story source: "Make Life an Adventure" by Roger Dawson, in Brian Cavanaugh (Ed.), *The Sower's Seeds,* New York: Paulist Press, 1990, #81, pp. 65-66.

Chapter 40

17th Sunday in Ordinary Time – C
Andy's Dream

Scripture:

- Genesis 18: 20-32
- Psalm 138: 1-2a, 2bcd-3, 6-7ab, 7c-8
- Colossians 2: 12-14
- Luke 11: 1-13

As we gather today to celebrate the Eucharist on this Seventeenth Sunday in Ordinary Time, we hear about the power of prayer. In the Old Testament selection from Genesis, for example, we learn that God does indeed listen to our prayers. In the Gospel reading, Jesus gives us an example of how to pray and tells us that our prayers will be answered to our satisfaction provided that what we are asking for will not harm us.

God always answers our prayers one-way or the other. "Yes," "no," or "later" are the usual answers. How he answers our prayers can be very interesting. That is what we see in the following story of a mother's prayer for her troubled teenage son, Andy, as told by Anne Bembry.

Anne would never forget the horrible feeling she had when she had to put her first-born son, Andy, into a juvenile detention center. He screamed, "I hate you! I never want to see you again!"

Anne's two other sons were very well behaved kids, but for some reason, Andy was trouble from the time he was in grade school. Anne and her husband Dan thought that with a little discipline and a lot of love, Andy would come around. But that never happened.

In fourth grade, the teachers diagnosed a learning disability in Andy and put him in a special class. Andy began skipping class for a month at a time. When confronted, he told his folks that he hated school. By age 13, he was hanging out with a wild crowd, smoking and fighting. Punishment, lectures, and therapy all did no good. In agony, Anne whispered the prayer, "Lord, help me!"

One night Andy was arrested for breaking into a home, just for kicks. But the thing that finally led Anne and Dan to take drastic action was when the guidance counselor told Andy's parents that Andy was contemplating suicide.

As a result of Andy's continuing destructive behavior, his parents put him into a juvenile center called Green Leaf. After one week there, the counselor from Green Leaf reported that Andy was breaking every rule, was hostile, and hated life. But then, one day, the counselor told Andy's parents that Andy was beginning to open up, and that his anger was disappearing.

Each week, Andy got better. He began to do well in class and had a bright attitude towards life and towards his parents and others around him. After four months in Green Leaf, he went home filled with joy. Soon he returned to school and was put in a regular class.

Anne was very grateful for the work Green Leaf did to help her son. It seemed an answer to her prayers. But about one year after Andy got home from Green Leaf, she learned a most amazing thing.

One evening, while the family was sitting around the fireplace, Andy said, "Mom, there's something I never told you."

He then began to share a dream he had at Green Leaf. In the dream, he was walking down a dirt road and came to an old house. There he saw an old woman sitting on the porch reading her Bible. Her white hair was tied up in a bun, and she was wearing a fringed shawl with some kind of diamond pattern on it.

When Andy asked her for a drink of water, she replied, "Andy, you are going the wrong way." He asked again for a drink of water, but she said, "Andy, I'm your great-grandmother. And you have got to change your ways."

Andy went on to tell his mom that the next day he began to change, to feel less angry. The dream stayed with him a long time.

Anne sobbed when she heard the story for indeed, what Andy described was his great-grandmother, whom he had never met. As the family listened, dumbstruck, Anne told them how her grandmother used to sit on the porch reading her Bible. She looked exactly as Andy reported in his dream. And the month before Andy was born, she had given Anne her favorite shawl with a diamond pattern. Andy had never seen this shawl, which had been stored away ever since her death.

Andy eventually grew up to be a fine young man and went on to serve his country in the National Guard. Anne's simple prayer, "Lord, help me!" was answered in a most dramatic and unusual manner.

In today's Gospel, Jesus teaches us some valuable things about prayer.

First, he teaches us a prayer that we know as "The Lord's Prayer" or the "Our Father." In it, we learn that we are to pray every day. This keeps us connected to God.

Second, even though God knows what we need before we ask, he wants us to ask for what we want and need. This helps to remind us that all good things come from him, that we are totally dependent upon him.

Third, we learn that just because we ask for something, God won't always give it to us. Perhaps the thing we ask for is not in harmony with the divine plan. So, just as a father would not give his child a scorpion if the child asks for an egg, so God will withhold something from us if it would not be in our best interest.

As we continue our life journeys this week, it would be a good idea to examine our own prayer lives. How does God answer our prayers? How many times has God not given us what we asked for, simply to give us something much nicer?

And that is the good news I have for you on this Seventeenth Sunday in Ordinary Time.

Story source: Anne Bembry, "Andy's Dream," in Canfield, Hansen, Aubery, & Mitchell (Eds.), *Chicken Soup for the Christian Soul*, 1997, pp. 144-147.

Chapter 41

18th Sunday in Ordinary Time – C
Remembered for What?

Scripture:

- Ecclesiastes 1: 2; 2: 21-23
- Psalm 90: 3-4, 5-6, 12-13, 14 & 17
- Colossians 3: 1-5, 9-11
- Luke 12: 13-21

As we come together to celebrate the Eucharist on this Eighteenth Sunday in Ordinary Time, we encounter two very interesting readings that make us think about basic values.

In the first reading from the Book of Ecclesiastes, we read, "All things are vanity!" (Ecclesiastes 1: 2). Although "vanity" today usually means boasting or prideful behavior, in the time Ecclesiastes was written, it meant "futility." Thus, the message was that all the things of this world are futile when compared to the next world.

And in the Gospel selection, we read of a farmer who was so successful that he decided to build larger barns to store up his abundant harvest. Then, he figured, he could sit back for years and "...rest, eat, drink, and be merry" (Luke 12: 19). That very night, however, he died. He was a fool, for he focused on the things of this world, things that meant nothing compared to his eternal life.

When we read such things in Sacred Scripture, we are forced to examine our own lives to see if our primary focus is on eternity or on the fleeting things of this world. That is what a management expert named Peter Drucker reflected on.

Peter recalled a question that one of his teachers, a priest, posed to his students when Peter was only thirteen years old. The teacher went through the class, stopped at each student, and asked, "What do you want to be remembered for?"

None of the students could answer that question. The teacher, then said, "I didn't expect you to be able to answer that question. However, if you still cannot answer that question by the time you are fifty years old, you will have wasted your life."

Sixty years passed, and Peter went to his sixtieth class reunion. One of his fellow students asked, "Do you remember Father Pflieger and that question?"

All of the students said they remembered the question well. Every one of them said it had made a big difference in their lives. They all said, however, that they really did not understand the question until they were in their forties. They reported that they began trying to answer the question when they were in their twenties, but the answers that they had come up with didn't last. It took them many more years to come up with an answer that really mattered.

Peter Drucker told the group that even now he continues to ask himself the question, "What do you want to be remembered for?" He said that when he asks himself that question, it pushes him to see himself as a different, better person, the person he *can become.*

Peter Drucker believes that youth are very fortunate if an authority figure such as a teacher asks them that question, for it will stay with them for the rest of their lives. And if they are like Peter, it will spur them on to never settle for what they are, but rather what they can become.

From the Scripture passages and Peter Drucker's reflections, we can gain the following three things.

First, when we hear "Vanity of vanity. All is vanity," we realize that all of the things of this world are fleeting or transitory. In my travels I often wander around cemeteries, for they are places where one is forced to remember one's mortality. And I can't help but notice how faded are many of the markings on the tombstones. I think of the worker who spent many hours carving names and dates and other inscriptions on the stone, only to have time gently erase the work that he did. Likewise, the material things we are so busy collecting are transitory in nature, for they are all subject to decay.

Second, when we hear that the things of this world are transitory or fleeting, we should not fall into a fundamentalist mode of regarding the world as intrinsically evil. On the contrary, the Catholic worldview is that the world and human beings are intrinsically good, for God created them. Likewise, our work is noble. In fact, at the Second Vatican Council, the Church Fathers reminded us that when we work we become "co-creators with God." So while the fruits of our labor may pass away as the markings of the tombstone engraver do, we should treasure our life work.

And third, we should store up things that matter. We should ask ourselves, "What do I want to be remembered for?" I would hope that none of us would say something like, "I want to be remembered for my excellent china collection" or "I want to be remembered for all the cars I collected" or "I want to be remembered for all the money I stored up in the bank."

Rather, we should strive for things that matter in eternity. Perhaps we want to be remembered as a gentle soul who walked through the world seeking peace. Maybe we want to be remembered as a person of great generosity, or who encouraged youth, or who brought laughter into world, or who was a champion for human rights, or who showed others how to suffer gracefully, or who served the poor and marginalized. The list is endless. And naturally, we all should want to be remembered as a holy person.

As we continue our life journeys this week, take some time and seriously think of this question: "What do I want to be remembered for?"

And that is the good news I have for you on this Eighteenth Sunday in Ordinary Time.

Story source: Anonymous, "To be remembered for what?" in Brian Cavanaugh (Ed.), *Sower's seeds of encouragement: Fifth planting,* New York: Paulist Press, 1998, #82, pp. 75-76.

Chapter 42

19th Sunday in Ordinary Time – C
If I Had to Do It Over

Scripture:

- Wisdom 18: 6-9
- Psalm 33: 1 & 12, 18-19, 20 & 22
- Hebrews 11: 1-2, 8-19
- Luke 12: 32-48

Today as we gather to celebrate the Eucharist on this Nineteenth Sunday in Ordinary Time, we hear Jesus reminding his followers that they do not know when their time on Earth will come to an end, so they should always be prepared for that day. We stay prepared, in large part, by living our lives in harmony with the Lord. We live our lives in faith: faith in God and faith that we are living our vocations in the light of God's grace.

Unfortunately, however, many people fail to live their lives to the fullest. Some people, for example, have lives that are boring and overly cautious instead of exciting, joyful, and robust. That is what the writer of the following essay is talking about. It is called "Brother Jeremiah and Christian Service."

> "If I had my life to live over again, I'd try to make more mistakes next time. I would relax. I would limber up. I would be sillier than I have been on this trip. I know of very few things I would take seriously. I would take more vacations. I would climb more mountains, swim more rivers, and watch more sunsets. I would do more walking and looking. I would eat more ice cream and less beans. I would have more actual troubles and fewer imaginary ones.
>
> "You see, I am one of those people who live preventively and sensibly and sanely, hour after hour, day after day. Oh, I've had my moments, and if I had to do it over again, I'd have more of them. In fact, I'd try to have nothing else. Just moments, one after another, instead of living so many years ahead each day. I have been one of those people who never goes anywhere without a thermometer, a hot water bottle, a gargle, a raincoat, aspirin, and a parachute. If I had it to do over again, I would go places, do things and travel lighter than I have.
>
> "If I had my life to live over, I would start barefoot earlier in the spring and stay that way later in the fall. I would play more. I would ride on more merry-go-rounds. I'd pick more daisies."

This beautiful piece of writing contains much wisdom. Many of us need to hear this message over and over again. Live life to the fullest!

Today we hear that we should live in such a way that when the Master calls us to heaven, we are ready. But many people are not making the most of their lives. Instead, they are merely "going through the motions" with one day being basically the same as the day before. There is rarely any change, any growth, any excitement. Why is this? After all, we are Catholic Christians. Of all the people on Earth, we should be living lives filled with joy. As Catholic Christians, we reject fundamentalism and all that entails. Instead, we are called to be people of the light. We are called to focus on goodness in God's creation, not on evil. We are called to be people of joy, not people of anger. We are called to bask in God's grace, that we see in every nook and cranny of our world, not spend our time complaining about the world's imperfections.

Here are just three common reasons why some Catholic Christians fail to live life to the fullest.

First, many have weak faith. They forget that God is watching over them, caring for them, loving them. Like the author who wrote about what he would do if he could live over again, they are overly cautious. Instead of simply taking prudent precautions, they go overboard in prevention. They build great walls around themselves so that no one can hurt them. The walls, instead of offering protection, become their individual prisons.

Second, some people cannot enjoy life because they get entangled in brambles. They get caught up in obsessions and lose their freedom. In our country, the biggest trap that can ensnare us is that of materialism. People who are trapped by this terrible spiritual malady find themselves in a continual search for more money, more power, more things, bigger houses, bigger cars, bigger and more expensive everything. For the greedy person, there will never be enough. And when there is never enough, one can never be filled with joy. One is always in a state of "lacking" instead of being in a state of "gratitude."

Finally, many people are simply in a rut. They lose their zest for excitement. They have no passion for things outside themselves. They begin to live lives of "quiet desperation." Every day is the same. There is no adventure.

Today we are called to be people of faith, to be people living our lives to the fullest, basking in the glory of God's grace that we see everywhere.

We are called to enter life with gusto. A bumper sticker I recently saw reflects this concept so well. It said, "Life is short. Eat biscuits."

How exciting is your life?

And that is the good news I have for you on this Nineteenth Sunday in Ordinary Time.

Story source: Anonymous, "Brother Jeremiah and Christian Service," in Brian Cavanaugh (Ed.), *The Sower's Seeds,* New York: Paulist Press, 1990, #51, pp. 42-43.

Chapter 43

20th Sunday in Ordinary Time – C
St. Wenceslas

Scripture:

- Jeremiah 38: 4-6, 8-10
- Psalm 40: 2, 3, 4, 18
- Hebrews 12: 1-4
- Luke 12: 49-53

Today as we gather to celebrate the Eucharist on this Twentieth Sunday in Ordinary Time, we receive some very disturbing and challenging news from Jesus in the Gospel of Luke.

In this Gospel passage, Jesus predicts that his coming on Earth will bring not peace, but conflict. Jesus says, "Do you think I have come to establish peace on the earth? No, I tell you, but rather division. From now on a household of five will be divided, three against two and two against three; a father will be divided against his son and a son against his father, a mother against her daughter and a daughter against her mother, a mother-in-law against her daughter-in-law and a daughter-in-law against her mother-in-law" (Luke 12: 51-53).

This message is indeed challenging for us, for like the Hebrew people of old, we would have liked Jesus to be a Prince of Peace. In fact, Christians often even name their parishes "Prince of Peace."

We see Jesus' prediction of conflict and division everywhere in the world. None of this is new. Conflict and division have always been present from the time the first human beings inhabited the planet. Oftentimes, the people of today think conflict and division are something new. They have the bizarre idea that the problems of the world are caused by people who don't think as they do. In their egocentric world, they believe that if everyone thought as they did, the world would be a perfect place. Such thinking is, indeed, delusional, for it will never happen.

Instead of engaging in wishful thinking, it is better to face the reality that Jesus was teaching us: conflict and division existed in the past, and will exist in the present. Deal with it.

But before looking at ways in which we can deal with conflict and division, let's look at a family that experienced just what Jesus was talking about. Then, we'll look at some of the things we can glean from the Scripture of today.

The portrait we examine today is that of a royal family in the Kingdom of Bohemia in the Tenth Century. The four main characters in this story were Wenceslas, his brother Boleslas, his mother Drahomira, and his grandmother Ludmila.

Wenceslas was born in the Bohemian capital of Prague in 907, the eldest son of the royal family. From an early age, his grandmother Ludmila took him under her wings and gave him a sound Catholic education.

Though Wenceslas' mother, Drahomira, was nominally Catholic, she was born a pagan and was not very involved in his upbringing as a Catholic Christian. This made for bad relations between Ludmila and Drahomira.

When Wenceslas was just 14 years old, his father died in battle. Drahomira, backed by anti-Christian forces, took control of the government and installed a very secularist regime.

When Ludmila began encouraging Wenceslas to begin grasping the reins of government, Drahomira's forces murdered Ludmila. That did not work, for Wenceslas became the duke. Wenceslas was a wise and prudent ruler. Soon, he got married and had a son, the new heir-apparent to the throne.

With the birth of Wenceslas' son, Boleslas became very jealous, for he wanted to rule Bohemia one day. Therefore, in September of 929, Boleslas invited his brother Wenceslas to celebrate the feast of Saints Cosmas and Damian and the dedication of a church there. At the celebration, people tried to warn Wenceslas that he was in danger, but he brushed aside the warnings.

The next morning, on his way to prayer, Wenceslas met his brother to thank him for his hospitality. In response to the thanks, Boleslas struck Wenceslas. While the brothers struggled, friends of Boleslas ran up and killed Wenceslas. Historians report that as he fell at the chapel door, Wenceslas said, "Brother, may God forgive you."

Today, both Wenceslas and his grandmother Ludmila are recognized saints of the Catholic Church. St. Wenceslas' feast day is September 28th, and St. Ludmila's feast day is September 18th. In parts of the United States where there were many Bohemian immigrants, many parishes are named after these two saints.

From the Scripture today, we can learn many things. Here are just three.

First, Jesus predicted that because he came as the messiah, there would be conflict and division on earth. No amount of wishful thinking will alter that stark fact.

Second, as Catholic Christians, we should strive to make this a better world. We do this by trying to put Christian commands into action. We practice the corporal and spiritual works of mercy. We strive to combat social evils such as poverty, prejudice, discrimination, violence, and the like. In other words, we strive to see Christ and each person and then act accordingly.

And third, even though Catholic Christians value harmony and unity, we must never compromise the triple love commandment of Jesus in the name of "Christian unity." We must never minimize, gloss over, or tolerate the anti-love rhetoric that some self-proclaimed "Christians" espouse. It is not acceptable to embrace hate in order to achieve unity. We must use our gifts of wisdom and prudence in evaluating what we experience, and then discard what is not in harmony with Christ's triple love command.

As we continue on our life journeys this week, it would be a good idea to reflect on our lives. What kind of conflict and division do we experience in our lives? How are we dealing with this?

And that is the good news I have for you on this Twentieth Sunday in Ordinary Time.

Story source: "St. Wenceslas," in *Butler's Lives of the Saints – September*, pp. 256-258.

Chapter 44

21st Sunday in Ordinary Time – C
Carving Heaven's Gate

Scripture:

- Isaiah 66: 18-21
- Psalm 117: 1, 2
- Hebrews 12: 5-7, 11-13
- Luke 13: 22-30

Today as we gather to celebrate the Eucharist on this Twenty-First Sunday in Ordinary Time, we hear Jesus talking about salvation. In his message, he reminds us that we are to follow him, "the narrow gate."

Jesus' teaching calls us to reflect on what we, as Catholic Christians, believe about the concept of salvation. Is salvation—which refers to going to heaven when we die—for everyone or just for a few? Catholic Christians believe it is for everyone.

But before exploring salvation from a Catholic Christian perspective, let's look at the following story.

There was once a woodsman and his son who lived by a large forest. The woodsman was a very hard worker, and the king had given him permission to cut all the wood that he needed for building, or making furniture, or fuel, or whatever he needed for his family. The woodsman worked very hard and made a good living, and he hoped that his son would follow in his footsteps and also become a woodsman.

The son, however, felt that being a woodsman was too much work. He decided instead to become a royal hunter, for that would be a much easier job.

One day, when the young man was out in the forest, he came upon a hermit's cabin. The hermit was very well known throughout the region because of the many kind deeds he was always doing for the poor. When the young man knocked on the hermit's door, the hermit greeted him warmly and invited the young man in. He treated the young man as though he were Jesus Christ himself, for that is how holy people always treat visitors.

After they had eaten, the hermit spent all afternoon telling the young man stories about great men and women who did wonderful things on Earth and were now saints in heaven. The young man was very impressed by the stories, and he asked the hermit if he could come back to hear more. The hermit readily agreed, on the condition that the young man never tell anyone where he lived. For, you see, the hermit did not want people to thank him for his good deeds, as he was very humble.

The young man continued to visit and learn about the saints throughout the summer. But when the first heavy snow of winter came, the hermit told the young man that he was going on a long journey and would never see him again on this earth. He prayed that one day they would meet again in heaven.

Before they said good-bye, the hermit gave the young man a gift, an exceedingly sharp knife. He said, "One day this may open heaven's gate for you." And the young man never saw the hermit again.

To make a long story short, the young man began to whittle wood at home with his magnificent knife, and then to carve magnificent statues of the saints the hermit had told him about. Thus, the young man became a wood carver and spent his years in this career.

Before he died, however, he decided to create a magnificent church carved out of wood. It was the most spectacular church ever created, for it was carved in a most intricate way. It was filled with statues and delicate latticework and ornate cornices. Then, as soon as it was complete, the carver died.

But when he got to heaven's gates, he could not get the doors open. He thought of using his knife as a key, but there was not even a hole. So the carver returned to earth.

When he got back to the forest, a heavy snowstorm was underway, and all the people were crowded into the church for warmth. But soon the firewood was gone, and the people began to cut down the statues to burn them to survive the bitter cold. Soon, the church was gone, and the man began to cry to see his life's work destroyed.

But suddenly he heard the sound of music, and he realized that he was once again at heaven's gate. With the slightest push, the gates of heaven opened, and there to greet him was the hermit and all the saints whom he had carved from wood. Jesus came to him and, with a smiling face, said, "Heaven's gate is opened only through suffering."

Today the Lord asks us in the Gospel story to follow the narrow path, that is, by following him. The message Jesus gives us today leads us to ask, "What do Catholic Christians believe about salvation?" Here are just a few of our beliefs.

First, salvation for Catholic Christians is more than going to heaven. Rather, it involves the restoration and fulfillment of the entire creation effected by God in Jesus Christ through the Holy Spirit. For the Catholic, salvation is the triumph over sin and death. It is God's greatest triumph.

Second, at every Mass, we ask God to grant salvation for all humanity because we believe that for God, all things are possible and that God's mercy has no limits. In celebration of the Eucharist, we bring all humanity to God the Father, through Jesus Christ, by the power of the Holy Spirit.

And third, Catholic Christians believe they must never judge the state of the soul of others. It is not ours to say, under any circumstances, that any particular person or group of persons will not achieve salvation. Salvation is God's own province.

As we continue our life journeys this week, it would be a good idea to ask ourselves if we, as Catholic Christians, have remembered to ask God for the salvation of all humanity in our daily prayers.

And that is the good news I have for you on this Twenty-First Sunday in Ordinary Time.

Story source: "Heaven's Gate," by John R. Aurelio, in John R. Aurelio (Ed.), *Colors! Stories of the Kingdom*, New York: Crossroad, 1993, #25, pp. 86-90.

Chapter 45

22nd Sunday in Ordinary Time – C
Humility & the Chicken Lady

Scripture:

- Sirach 3: 17-18, 20, 28-29
- Psalm 68: 4-5ac, 6-7ab, 10-11
- Hebrews 12: 18-19, 22-24a
- Luke 14: 1, 7-14

Today as we gather to celebrate the Eucharist on this Twenty-Second Sunday in Ordinary Time, we hear a very clear message in both the Old Testament and Gospel readings about the virtue of humility.

In the Gospel reading, for example, Jesus tells a parable about how we should always be ready to take the lower places when we are invited to a banquet, and in the reading from Sirach, we read, "My child, conduct your affairs with humility, and you will be loved more than a giver of gifts" (Sirach 3: 17). Sirach then goes on to say, "Humble yourself the more, the greater you are, and you will find favor with God" (Sirach 3: 18).

Humbling oneself when one has a high position in society is not always easy. That is what one United States Governor once discovered.

Christian Herter was the Governor of Massachusetts, and he was running for re-election. When American politicians run for political office, they attend many events where food is served so they can meet the people.

One day, Governor Herter arrived late at a barbeque dinner. Because of his busy schedule, he had not had breakfast or lunch, and he was famished. As he moved down the serving line, he held out his plate for some chicken. The woman behind the table put one piece of chicken on his plate. The Governor said to the serving lady, "Madam, do you mind if I get another piece of chicken? I'm very hungry."

The woman replied, "I'm very sorry, but I have strict orders to give only one piece of chicken to each person." The Governor again said, "But I'm starving!" Again, the woman said, "Sorry, only one to a customer." The Governor was a humble sort of man, so he did not like to "throw his weight around" and get things simply because of his high office. But today he was so hungry, he decided to be a "big shot" to get his way. He said, "Madam, do you know who I am? I am the Governor of this state." The woman replied, "And do you know who I am? I am the lady in charge of the chicken. Move along, mister."

Like the Governor in this story, we too sometimes forget to be humble. We think we're better than others and should, therefore, be treated as more special than others. We fail at humility.

A virtue is a good habit that allows us to perform actions with ease. Therefore, the more we practice a virtue, the more embedded it becomes in us. Humility is no exception. It is the virtue in which we know our place and gratefully take it. St. Thomas Aquinas, the ultimate expert on virtues, said that humble people are balanced, that is, they do not get prideful about their talents, but on the other hand, they do not undervalue themselves.

The opposite of a virtue is a vice, and there are three vices that are obstacles to humility. By knowing these enemies of humility, we can watch out for them and weed them out of the garden of our soul. Three common enemies of the virtue of humility are arrogance, false humility, and judgmentalism.

Arrogance is oftentimes seen when people continually boast about themselves. Instead of realizing that their accomplishments could only have been achieved by the gifts that God gave them, they brag about themselves. Often such people insist on being the center of attention. When they are not, they no longer want to be around the people who are not letting them be the center of attention.

A second enemy of true humility is a condition called "false humility." People who engage in "false humility" often believe they are intrinsically terrible people. They fail to appreciate that they are children of God, and that God loves them deeply. Instead of having a balanced spirituality, they focus on their sins instead of the good things they do. At one point in Church history, this kind of thinking was actually encouraged, and people did very negative things such as self-mutilation and staying away from Holy Communion because they felt unworthy.

Another kind of false humility is actually a method of "fishing for compliments." The straight-A student, for example, often will say how they are sure they are going to fail an exam. They don't for a minute believe that. Rather, they want the listener to boost their ego by saying something like, "Oh, no, you're bound to get a high grade because you're the smartest person in the class!" This type of false humility is actually a form of pride.

And finally, judgmentalism is a third enemy of humility. Judgmental persons see themselves as morally superior to other people. They see themselves as holier and wiser. Frequently they engage in pious practices that others around them are not doing, thus making themselves the center of attention. When they do this at celebrations such as Eucharist, they distract others by their behavior, thus taking the focus off of the Blessed

Sacrament onto their own personal, self-centered behaviors. All the while, however, they imagine themselves to be superior.

As we continue our life journey this week, it would be a good idea to examine our own lives to see how we are cultivating the virtue of humility.

And that is the good news I have for you on this Twenty-Second Sunday in Ordinary Time.

Story source: "The Chicken Lady," in William J. Bausch (Ed.), *A World of Stories for Preachers and Teachers,* Mystic, CT: Twenty-Third Publications, 1998, #323, p. 385.

Chapter 46

23rd Sunday in Ordinary Time – C
Detachment and the Gem

Scripture:

- Wisdom 9: 13-18b
- Psalm 90: 3-4, 5-6, 12-13, 14 & 17
- Philemon 9-10, 12-17
- Luke 14: 25-33

As we come to together to celebrate the Eucharist on this Twenty-Third Sunday in Ordinary Time, we hear Jesus tell his disciples some very strange things. First, he tells them that they must hate their family members. Then he tells them they must take up their cross and follow him. And third, he tells them that anyone who does not renounce all his possessions cannot be his disciple.

Fortunately for Catholic Christians, we are not Biblical literalists. We do not believe that we are to actually hate people and give away everything we own. Rather, we look for the primary message Jesus is trying to tell us in his very powerful verbal images.

When we examine this Gospel passage, we come to the conclusion that Jesus is simply telling us that we must be detached from people and things to the extent that we can put Jesus first in our lives. Everyone and everything else is secondary. But before looking more closely at this Gospel selection, let us look at a story illustrating the concept of detachment.

There was once a young man who found the most beautiful and expensive gem in the entire world. He kept it in his pocket. Whenever people would come up to the young man and ask to see the gem, he gladly showed it to them.

Unfortunately, though, there was a thief who very much wanted the gem. In thinking of how he could get the gem away from the young man, he came up with a plan. First, he would simply demand that the young man turn the gem over to him. If that didn't work, he would kill the young man and steal the gem.

With his plan firmly in mind, the thief came up to the young man as he was out walking one day. "Give me the precious gem you carry around with you!" demanded the thief. "I want it!"

The young man calmly replied, "Oh, certainly. Here you are." With those words, he turned over the gem and happily continued his walk.

The thief was astonished at how easily the young man gave away the gem. Instead of making him happy, however, he was troubled. Why did the young man turn over the gem so readily? That night, the thief had nothing but nightmares.

The following day, the thief had a flash of insight. He rushed to find the young man. When he found him, the thief said, "Young man, I thought I would treasure the gem you gave me. However, I have discovered that you possess something even more valuable than the gem. What I would like is the same ability to be detached from the things of this world that you possess. I am amazed at how happy you were even though you lost a precious gem. Your spirit of detachment is what I really want. You may have your gem back."

Of all the stories I know, and I know plenty of them, this is one of the most powerful and meaningful to me. It also fits the Gospel message we hear today perfectly.

In today's Gospel selection, Jesus talks about the concept of detachment in three different ways.

First, he tells his disciples that they are to put him above even their families and their own lives. Does this mean we are to despise our families? On the contrary, we are supposed to love everyone in this world, including our families. Does this mean we are to see human life as not very important? Of course not; we are to treasure our lives. However, if we are called to give our life for our faith, we should be able to do that. We have thousands and thousands of examples of heroes who gave their lives for the faith. They are called martyrs. As followers of Christ, even human life must be secondary to our love of Christ.

Second, another way that Jesus calls for us to be detached from things of this world is by instructing us always to be ready to carry our crosses. This means that we should not strive to find the easier, softer way in life. Rather, sometimes following Jesus requires us to make sacrifices. For example, many people would like to spend every penny they make on themselves and their own gratification. But as followers of Christ, we know that is selfish. We need to spend some of our earnings on caring for the less fortunate. The same is true of our time. Instead of using all of our free time for our own selfish pleasures, we need to use some of it to serve others and to worship the Lord.

And finally, Jesus talks about detachment from the things of this world by saying, "…anyone of you who does not renounce all his possessions cannot be my disciple" (Luke 14: 33). Does this mean we have to get rid of all our material things to be a follower of Jesus? No. It means, instead, that we should not be so attached to the things of this world that we put them before Jesus. What Jesus was doing was using a "figure of speech," not a literal command. Jesus used other figures of speech to get his message across, such as saying we need to proclaim our faith from the housetops. He did not mean we needed to literally get on roofs of houses to preach. Rather, he meant we should make our message known to the whole world.

As we continue of our life journeys this week, it would be a good idea to see how detached we are from the things of the world. Do we own our possessions, or do they own us?

And that is the good news I have for you on this Twenty-Third Sunday in Ordinary Time.

Story source: Unknown.

Chapter 47

24ᵗʰ Sunday in Ordinary Time – C
Ribbons & Forgiveness

Scripture:

- Exodus 32: 7-11, 13-14
- Psalm 51: 3-4, 12-13, 17 & 19
- 1 Timothy 1: 12-17
- Luke 15: 1-32

As we come together to celebrate the Eucharist on this Twenty-Fourth Sunday in Ordinary Time, we encounter three stories of Jesus in the Gospel selection from Luke.

Jesus was always telling stories to teach basic principles. Some of his stories were agricultural stories such as that of the mustard seed that grew up to be so large that birds came into it to build their homes. Others were food stories such as how adding yeast to flour can produce much change. Some stories were what we call the "good guy versus bad guy" kind of stories, such as by contrasting humble and arrogant persons. Finally, there is the lost-and-found story, and today we encounter three of them in our Gospel selection: the lost sheep; the lost coin; and the Prodigal Son.

Whenever we hear lost-and-found stories from Jesus, we need to remember that the focus is not on the "lost" part of the story, but rather on the "found" part. Many of Jesus' stories end on a happy note, on a "good news" note. That is what we see in the following story re-told by Alice Gray.

There was once a handsome young man in his twenties who was traveling alone on a bus. Occasionally, he would look away from the window with anxiety on his face, and an occasional tear would fall from his eyes. A grandmother sitting nearby noticed the young man's anxiety, and it touched her heart. So she left her seat on the other side of the bus and sat next to him.

After some small talk, the young man told the grandmother about how he had been in prison for two years and had just gotten out that morning. He told the woman how his family was very poor and did not have much of an education. They were, however, a proud family, and his crime had brought shame and heartache to his parents. In the two years he had been in prison, he had not heard from his family at all. He knew that they were too poor to travel the distance to visit the prison, and he knew that his parents probably felt too uneducated to write. After a while, he had stopped writing them.

Three weeks before he was to be released, however, he wrote one more letter. He told them how sorry he was for disappointing them, and he asked for their forgiveness.

He then wrote how he was going to be released from prison, and that the bus he would be on would go right past their house. He said that he would understand if they did not forgive him.

He wanted to make it easy for his parents, so he gave them a signal they could use that he could see from the bus. If they had forgiven him and wanted him home, they should tie a white ribbon on the old apple tree that stood in the front yard. If the signal did not appear, he would stay on the bus, leave town, and be out of their lives forever.

As the bus neared the street where his parents lived, he became so anxious that he could not look out the window. The grandmother, after listening to his touching story, asked, "Would it help if we traded seats? I'll sit by the window and look out for you." He readily agreed. After a few more blocks, the grandmother touched the young man's shoulder and, choking back tears, she said, "Look! The whole tree is covered with white ribbons!"

This is a very beautiful story about forgiveness, the theme of today's gospel. From this story, as well as those that Jesus told in the Gospel, we can learn at least three things.

First, we should not dwell on the past. The past is gone. It is history. The mistakes we made in our lives are not permanent in nature; rather, they are transitory. We can always make up for our mistakes. Instead of re-living the mistakes of our past, we should focus on the present and on the future. Beating ourselves up over past mistakes or sins does no good. In fact, we could be violating the third part of the Triple Love Commandment that is the foundation of our Catholic Christian Faith: to love ourselves.

Second, like the father in the story of the Prodigal Son, and like the parents of the young man coming home from prison, God is always willing to forgive us. God's mercy is limitless. For the Catholic Christian, the graces that flowed from Christ's death and resurrection are sufficient for all humanity, not just for a select few. That is why Catholic Christians pray for the salvation of all humanity. We do not worship a weak God, and we do not consider Christ's death and resurrection impotent events. Rather, we see the divine graces of love and mercy to be without limit.

And third, these stories call each of us to imitate Christ. Just as we want God to be merciful and forgiving towards us, we are called to be merciful and forgiving towards others. Everyone makes mistakes; that is part of our human frailty. And in the back of our minds, we remember that Jesus told us that how we forgive others is exactly how we will be forgiven. With this piece of information, we should each try to be giants in the field of forgiveness and mercy.

As we continue our life journeys this week, it would be a good idea to examine our own lives. Are we willing to forgive others? Are we champions of mercy?

And that is the good news I have for you on this Twenty-Fourth Sunday in Ordinary Time.

Story source: Alice Gray, "The Signal," in *Stories for the Heart: 110 Stories to Encourage Your Soul,* Gresham, Oregon: Vision House, Compiled by Alice Gray, 1996, pp. 83-84.

Chapter 48

25th Sunday in Ordinary Time – C
A Pat of Butter

Scripture:

- Amos 8: 4-7
- Psalm 113: 1-2, 4-6, 7-8
- 1 Timothy 2: 1-8
- Luke 16: 1-13

On this Twenty-Fifth Sunday in Ordinary Time, Catholic Christians throughout the world are asked to celebrate the work that our catechists do for the Church. Although all Catholic Christians are called to spread their Faith, catechists have special preparation to teach the Faith to children, youth, and adults. Therefore, they are very treasured people in our parishes.

Catechists not only transmit knowledge of our Catholic Christian faith, but they also strive to help others develop virtues in their lives. This is especially important for children and youth. Virtues, as you remember, are habits, and habits are strengthened only by practice. Good catechists not only help their students develop and practice virtues, they also try to make themselves living homilies, demonstrating virtues by the way they live. The role of catechist is, therefore, a very noble one.

In today's Gospel selection, Jesus talks about a virtue called trustworthiness. In the Gospel passage, Jesus says, "The person who is trustworthy in very small matters is also trustworthy in great ones; and the person who is dishonest in very small matters is also dishonest in great ones" (Luke 16: 10). Catechists take such a virtue, explain it, and give some examples of how it can be lived. That is what we will do now.

Once there were four young men who were all competing to become the head of the trust department at a bank. After interviews and weighing the qualities of each candidate, the board of directors made a decision to hire one of the young men. They decided that they would tell the young man about their decision to hire him after they had lunch. The young man would not only have a new job, but he would also have a fine raise in pay.

During the noon hour, the young man who had been chosen went through the cafeteria line. One of the directors was behind him in the line, separated by a few other customers. The director saw the young man select his food, including a small pat of butter. As the young man neared the cashier's station, he covered the pat of butter with his napkin so he would not have to pay for it.

After lunch, the board of directors met to notify the young man of their decision to hire him. But before asking the young man to come into the conference, the director who had seen the young man hide his butter told the other directors about his observation. Therefore, instead of giving the young man the promotion, they called him in and fired him.

They felt that if the young man were willing to lie to a cashier about what was on his plate, he would be just as willing to lie about what was in the bank's accounts. The board of directors was following the principle that Jesus was talking about: if one is dishonest in small things, one cannot be trusted with big things.

But how do we show trustworthiness in everyday life? Here are three ways we show that we are trustworthy persons.

First, trustworthy persons show up when they are supposed to show up. The comedian Woody Allen famously said, "Ninety percent of life is just showing up." There is a great deal of truth to that statement. All of us know people who say that they will come to a meeting or help with a project, but on the day of the meeting or project, they fail to show up. I'm not talking about being unable to show up due to an emergency. I'm talking about people who make a pattern of this.

In parish life, for example, we often keep lists of people scheduled for a specific event. People volunteer to help on a project or perform some ministry at Mass. When a person doesn't show up, others may say, "Oh, that person never shows up" or "That person is always late." But they will say of a trustworthy person, "That's very unusual. Usually they are here if they say they'll be here. They must be sick."

Second, trustworthy people do what they say they will do. Not only do they show up for a task, they will actually do what they promised. You can count on such people. Trustworthy persons do not need much supervision, for they work whether someone is watching them or not. This is the mark of a trustworthy person. This is what separates the "talkers" from the "doers."

Finally, trustworthy persons are not afraid to do the little things and get their hands dirty. I remember, for example, visiting with a priest one day when I was a seminarian. As we walked along, he bent over to pick up a piece of paper from the sidewalk. He said, "This is a piece of paper that only pastors can see." At the time I didn't understand what he was saying. Today I do understand it. I can't tell you how many times there are little pieces of trash littering our campus. Sometimes I just watch to see how long it will stay there. Finally, after hundreds of people have walked by without picking it up, and several days go by, I pick it up and throw it away.

This week, as we continue our life journeys, it would be a good idea to examine our own lives. Are we trustworthy people? Do we do what we say we will do? Can people count on us?

That is the good news I have for you on this Twenty-Fifth Sunday in Ordinary Time.

<u>Story source:</u> *God's Little Devotional Book for Men,* Honor Books, 1996, pp. 26-27.

Chapter 49

26th Sunday in Ordinary Time – C
Generosity & the Queen's Table

Scripture:

- Amos 6: 1a, 4-7
- Psalm 146: 6c-7, 8-9a, 9bc-10
- 1 Timothy 6: 11-16
- Luke 16: 19-31

As we gather to celebrate the Eucharist on this Twenty-Sixth Sunday of Ordinary Time, we encounter some very stark reminders about how important it is to be generous with what we have. These reminders from the prophet Amos, the psalmist, and the Gospel of Luke are all foundations for the Catholic social teaching that we, as Catholic Christians, are taught to put into action.

Although every one of us knows that we are to be generous with what God has blessed us with, sometimes we can be stingy. We can avoid helping those in need, making up all sorts of excuses or rationalizations in our minds to justify our stinginess. Unfortunately, we forget that our lack of generosity does have consequences, as the people in the following story found out the hard way.

There was once a kind and generous queen who cared deeply for the poor, the sick, and the outcasts of her kingdom. One day, though, she heard some disturbing news: many people of the realm were getting very selfish and not caring for those who were less fortunate than they were. To see just how serious the problem was, she decided to go and see for herself.

To test the charity of the neighbors, the queen disguised herself as a poor woman and went begging in the streets for food. At some houses, the people gave her things of little value such as rotten onions, moldy bread or rotten fruit. At other houses, she was given nothing at all except harsh words and angry looks.

There was only one place in the neighborhood where she was treated with dignity and respect, where she was treated as Christ. That place was a little cottage that belonged to a poor man. He welcomed her with kindness and invited her to sit by the fire. There he served her a warm meal and talked and laughed with her. She enjoyed the poor man's company so much, in fact, that she stayed there over an hour.

The next day, all of the people whom the queen had visited received a surprise invitation to the castle for a banquet. When the guests arrived, servants of the palace led them to the dining room. Place cards showed where each guest was to sit at the table. On the plate in front of each guest was the same thing that person had given to the disguised queen the day before - rotten onions, moldy bread, rotten fruit, or nothing at all. Only the poor man was served a plate full of delicious food.

Suddenly, the queen entered the dining room and explained to the guests, "Yesterday, to test your charity, I went about the village disguised as a beggar woman. As you notice, today I am serving you the same thing you served me yesterday."

When we hear such a story, it's natural to ask ourselves, "What would I be served? Would I be like the poor man who recognized Christ in the queen-disguised-as-a-beggar? Or would I be sitting at the table with an empty plate?

The moral of this story, as well as the moral of the Scripture passages today, is that generosity is God's command to us. Here are three points that we can make about the virtue of generosity.

First, everything that we have is a gift from God. That includes not only our health and family and friends and the beautiful world around us, but also such intangible things as our enthusiasm, work ethic, energy, and opportunities that we have by living in this society.

Second, all gifts from God are social in nature. In other words, God never gives us gifts to be hoarded. Rather, all gifts are designed to share with others. As Catholic Christians, we are called to share our time, talent, and treasure, especially with those less fortunate than ourselves and those in need. We are called to be champions of the underdogs of society. We are called to be their advocates by recognizing that Christ lives in each and every human being on the planet.

Catholic Christians have an abundance of opportunities to practice generosity. We are called by Catholic teaching to support our parish, but we also have many other opportunities. We have many second collections during the year, for example, for the special needs of the Church in various parts of the world or for various populations. We have opportunities to give to the missions at home and abroad. This weekend, for example, we are asked to show our generosity to Catholic Charities.

Catholic Charities in the Diocese of Raleigh, for example, serves over 54,000 people each year. By seeing Christ in every human person, especially in the poor, the sick, and the suffering, Catholic Charities supports the life and dignity of each person. It not only "talks the talk," but it "walks the walk." Whether it is feeding the poor, doing marriage counseling, helping those made homeless by hurricanes, or welcoming immigrants, Catholic Charities takes our donations and puts them to good use.

And the third point about generosity is that *now* is the time to be generous. When we are dead, it is too late. That is the radically stark image that Jesus was telling in the story of Lazarus and the rich man.

As we continue our life journeys this week, it would be good to ask ourselves, "What would I be served at the queen's banquet?"

And that is the good news I have for you on this Twenty-Sixth Sunday in Ordinary Time.

Story source: Unknown

Chapter 50

27th Sunday in Ordinary Time – C
Guerillas, Faith, & Respect

Scripture:

- Habakkuk 1: 2-3; 2: 2-4
- Psalm 95: 1-2, 6-7c, 7d-9
- 2 Timothy 1: 6-8, 13-14
- Luke 17: 5-10

Today as we come to celebrate the Eucharist on this Twenty-Seventh Sunday in Ordinary Time, also known as Respect Life Sunday, we hear about the concept of "faith" in all of the readings.

The Old Testament prophet Habakkuk tells us that the "rash man has no integrity; but the just man, because of his faith, shall live" (Habakkuk 2: 4). St. Paul, in his second letter to Timothy, tells Timothy not to be afraid of proclaiming this faith. And Jesus tells us in the Gospel of Luke, "If you had faith the size of a mustard seed, you would say to this mulberry tree, 'Be uprooted and planted in the sea,' and it would obey you" (Luke 17: 6).

Faith is the unquestioning belief in things we cannot see. For the Catholic Christian, our faith leads us to believe in the Blessed Trinity and many other things. But faith can sometimes be taken for granted. It can diminish over time when we don't put it into action. When we are not challenged, it can become so weak that we can lose it altogether. That is what happened to some of the people in the following story.

It was a typical Sunday morning in South America. Catholic Christians had gathered in their little chapel on the border of Venezuela and Colombia for Mass. But as soon as the Mass began, something truly amazing and terrifying occurred: a band of guerillas, armed with machine guns, came out of the jungle and crashed their way into the little chapel. Needless to say, the priest and congregation were quite frightened by the guerillas and their guns.

First the guerillas dragged the priest outside the chapel to be executed. Then the leader of the guerillas came back into the chapel and demanded, "Anyone else who believes in this God stuff, come forward!" Everyone was petrified and stood frozen in place. But after a long silence, a man came forward and said, "I love Jesus." The soldiers treated him very roughly and then took him outside to be executed with the priest. Then others began to come forward and proclaim their faith, and the soldiers took them outside to be killed.

Soon the people who were still inside the chapel, those who had not come forward to proclaim their faith, heard the sound of machine gun fire outside the chapel. When the gunfire was over, the guerilla leader came back inside the chapel and told the remaining congregation to get out. "You have no right to be here!" With that, the guerilla leader herded the faithless Christians out of the chapel, where they were astonished to see their priest and the faithful Christians standing there safe and sound.

The guerilla leader then ordered the priest and the faithful ones of the congregation back into the chapel to resume celebrating the Mass. To those who had refused to proclaim their faith, however, the guerilla leader angrily warned them to stay out of the chapel until they had the courage to stand up for their beliefs! And with that admonition, the band of guerillas disappeared into the jungle once again.

If you are like most people, you are probably sitting there wondering, "If I had been in that little congregation, would my faith be stronger than my fear? Or would I have been one of the people whose fear overcame my faith?" Naturally, we would all hope that we would have been people whose faith would have won.

In Catholic Christianity, we are asked today to reflect on a basic part of our faith, namely that all people are created in the image of God. Therefore, all people are our brothers and sisters. Thus, we are to treat all with dignity and respect.

In looking at our world, though, it is easy to be discouraged. We see so many instances of a lack of respect for human life—both physical life and the life of the human spirit. We wonder how God can allow anti-life forces to exist and sometimes flourish. Some of the more obvious forces set out to destroy the human spirit or physical life of human beings include poverty, racism, anti-male and anti-female sexism, war, hunger, induced abortion, active euthanasia, homophobia, environmental destruction, violence, imprisonment, joblessness, homelessness, genocide, untreated diseases, and a host of other maladies.

Instead of being lights to the world and trying to combat the enemies of the human spirit, however, many people simply make matters worse. Instead of trying to figure out causes of problems so they can come up with solutions, they adopt their own attitudes of hate and intolerance. They become disrespectful of anything and anyone with whom they disagree. They begin to divide the world into "good guys" and "bad guys," with themselves, of course, being the "good guys." Their hate can become so intense that any cooperation with others to make this a better world becomes impossible.

Followers of Jesus Christ are supposed to put their faith into action for good, not evil. Jesus told us that the very foundation of our faith is the triple love commandment: to love God, to love others, as we love ourselves. Anything less is not acceptable. The big challenge, however, is to love others even when they have different perspectives from us, when their priorities are different from ours.

As we continue our life journeys this week, it would be a good idea to examine our own faith and how we put it into action. Do we go through the world trying to see Christ in every human being and acting accordingly? Or do we go through the world filled with rage and hate toward those of God's children who appear different from us?

That is the good news I have for you on this Twenty-Seventh Sunday in Ordinary Time.

Story source: "The Guerilla," in William J. Bausch (Ed.), *A World of Stories for Preachers and Teachers,* Mystic, CT: Twenty-Third Publications, 1998, # 121, pp. 271-272.

Chapter 51

28th Sunday in Ordinary Time – C
The Doctor's Coat

Scripture:

- 2 Kings 5: 14-17
- Psalm 98: 1, 2-3ab, 3cd-4
- 2 Timothy 2: 8-13
- Luke 17: 11-19

As we come together to celebrate the Eucharist on this Twenty-Eighth Sunday in Ordinary Time, we hear the famous story of Jesus and the ten lepers.

In this story, Jesus cures ten lepers that he encountered on a journey. When they asked him to have pity on them, Jesus cured them. Only one of the lepers, however, returned to Jesus to thank him for this miracle. The one who returned was a Samaritan, someone that the Jewish people of the day did not like.

The moral of the story is, of course, that we are to be thankful for what we have. As we remember in Mass, every good thing comes from God. Sometimes, though, we need to remind ourselves just how blessed we are. That is what a physician learned in the following story.

There was once a young medical intern in New York City. One very cold, blustery, wintry night, a young girl came banging on the door to his apartment. She was very frightened and begged him to come to her home. After putting on his jacket, he followed the girl to a dirty, stinking tenement building. After going up a flight of very dark and dirty stairs, he entered a one-room apartment. There he found a desperately sick and malnourished little boy. The boy's mother and father were hovering over him. The intern did what he could for the little one, but the boy died right in front of him.

The intern was shivering not only from the loss of the child, but also because there was no heat in the apartment. The boy's father noticed how cold the intern was. He took off his coat and gave it to the intern saying, "Here, you're cold. Thank you for trying to save our little boy."

The intern knew that the shabby coat was the only tangible way the young couple could thank him. Therefore, he did not have the heart to give it back.

Years went by, and the intern became a prominent and wealthy physician. Every year, though, he takes out the dirty, shabby coat and wears it on two days: the anniversary of the boy's death and the anniversary of the day he got his diploma to practice medicine. He wears the coat to remind him what his profession is all about. It also helps him to remember not only to be grateful but also to accept gratitude from others.

From the Scripture and from this story, we learn that gratitude does not exist in a vacuum. Gratitude, like many other virtues, is related to other virtues. People who have an attitude of gratitude usually exhibit at least three other characteristics.

First, people who are grateful for what they have tend to have serenity or a sense of peace. Because they are content with what they have, they can enjoy what they have. They are not on an endless search for more and more and more. People who are not grateful for what they have, on the other hand, are never at peace. They are in an endless search for more things to fill up the empty holes in their spirits. Nothing is ever enough for those people, and so their never-ending quest for things they do not have consumes them. They do not have serenity like those who are very contented with what they have.

Second, people who are grateful are people of generosity. The two virtues are companions. People who are grateful realize that their gifts are from God, and God never gives us gifts to be hoarded. They realize, that what they have is to be shared with those who are in need.

That principle is seen in the story of Jesus curing the lepers and in the story of the young physician. The father of the dying boy, for example, was so grateful that he took off his shabby coat and gave it to the doctor. The doctor, in turn, used his medical gifts to share with others down the line.

Sometimes people are grateful for what they have, but allow obstacles to come between themselves and those in need. They buy into the false notion that they actually "own" things. No, we really don't "own" things, for we will leave this world one day, and we will not be able to take our "things" with us. The only things that will come with us into the next world are our soul and our glorified body. Therefore, the things we supposedly "own" are, at best, being "rented." When we forget this, we are endangering our gratitude and generosity.

And third, gratitude is helpful for our mental health. In the documents of the Second Vatican Council, the Church leaders told us that we are to use and treasure the findings of the various sciences—social, behavioral, and physical. Recent scientific studies have shown that grateful people tend to have less depression and stress in their lives compared to those who are not satisfied with what they have. Further, grateful people tend to have higher levels of alertness, enthusiasm, determination, optimism, and energy. They also tend to make more progress toward accomplishing personal goals.

In sum, gratitude is a very important virtue with many excellent consequences.

As we continue our life journeys this week, it would be a good idea to take some time to reflect on this question: How grateful am I for the things that God has given me?

And that is the good news I have for you on this Twenty-Eighth Sunday in Ordinary Time.

Story source: "The Doctor's Coat," in William J. Bausch (Ed.), *A World of Stories for Preachers and Teachers,* Mystic, CT: Twenty-Third Publications, 1998, #204, p. 326.

Chapter 52

29th Sunday in Ordinary Time – C
St. André Bessett

Scripture:

- Exodus 17: 8-13
- Psalm 121: 1-2, 3-4, 5-6, 7-8
- 2 Timothy 3: 14 – 4: 2
- Luke 18: 1-8

As we gather to celebrate the Eucharist on this Twenty-Ninth Sunday in Ordinary Time, also known as World Mission Sunday, we remember that all Catholic Christians are responsible for spreading the Faith. On this day, we take up a second collection for those on the front lines in poor mission territories who need our support.

In today's Gospel reading from Luke, Jesus talks of the virtue of perseverance, something every missionary needs. This is the virtue that allows us to continue living our vocations every day, through good times and bad, and never giving up. It is a virtue to which all Christians are called.

Today, Catholic Christians throughout the world are celebrating the canonization of a humble man who persevered in his vocation for many decades. That man was Alfred Bessette, later known as Brother André, a Holy Cross Brother who lived in both the United States and Canada.

Alfred was the eighth of twelve children born to a French Canadian couple near Montreal. He was adopted at the age of twelve when his parents died, and became a farmhand. He also had many other jobs as he grew up including shoemaker, baker, and blacksmith. He worked in the United States during the Civil War. Unfortunately, none of these jobs worked out for Alfred.

When he was twenty-five, he entered the Congregation of the Holy Cross. After a year, his superiors told him he did not have a vocation because of his weak health. However, a bishop intervened and coaxed the Order into giving André (which was his name in Religious Life) another chance. That they did, and André lived a humble but remarkable life as a Brother until his death at the age of ninety-two.

The Congregation gave Brother André the humble job as doorkeeper at Notre Dame College in Montreal, where he also served as a laundry worker, sacristan, and messenger.

But though he did these jobs very well, he was most famous for his nursing and the fact that God used him as his instrument to cure people.

When he heard that someone was sick, Brother André would take some oil from the lamp in the college chapel and anoint the sick person. Many were cured. Soon his reputation began to spread, and people sought him out. Brother André, who had a great love for St. Joseph, called his oil "St. Joseph's oil."

When an epidemic broke out at a local college, Brother André volunteered as a nurse. Not one of his patients died.

Besides healing the sick, Brother André also was successful in buying some land called Mount Royal. Though his Congregation could not talk the owner into selling it to them, Brother André climbed the hill and planted medals of St. Joseph, and soon the owners changed their minds.

Later, the Holy Cross Order built a chapel there, and soon it began to collect crutches, canes, and braces of those cured after seeing Brother André. When the Order wanted to build a bigger chapel to hold all the people who were coming, Brother André buried a statue of St. Joseph and said, "If he wants a roof over his head, he'll get it." Though it took fifty years to build, the Oratory of St. Joseph in Montreal is one of the largest churches in the world. Its walls are covered with crutches, canes, and braces.

By the time of his death, Brother André needed four secretaries to handle the 80,000 letters he received from around world each year.

Brother André died in 1937 and was canonized on October 17, 2010.

What a remarkable man he was, yet what simple virtues he demonstrated. Humility, love, compassion, sensitivity, resilience, patience, and many others are easy to spot. Yet underneath all of his virtues was the virtue of perseverance, the virtue that Jesus is extolling in today's Gospel passage.

Perseverance is the quality of moving forward no matter what. Sometimes the journey is easy, and everything is going our way. We may have great health, a bright outlook, people who love us, a steady job, and a future filled with nothing but sunshine and rainbows. But other times, our life journeys may be hard, and we find ourselves in what the psalmist calls "the dark valley." Instead of seeing sunshine and rainbows, it is easier to see clouds and storms.

Perseverance, however, allows us to walk forward each day, one step at a time. It allows us to face the world with courage and hope and faith. Perseverance reminds us that we are to live our vocations as best we can whether we feel like it or not. I remember a monk from St. Meinrad Archabbey in Indiana. He said that being a monk is not at all difficult, for just about anybody can do it. He said what makes a monk worthy of praise is not his daily life, but rather, that he lives his life day after day after day for his faith until death. It is the perseverance that is praiseworthy, not the tasks of being a monk. And can't the same be said for any vocation?

As we continue our life journey this week, it would be a good idea to examine our own perseverance. Are we people who can be counted on to live our vocation to the best of our ability no matter what life throws at us? Or do we crumble when the storms of life find us?

And that is the good news I have for you on this 29th Sunday in Ordinary Time.

Story sources:

- "Blessed Andrew Bessette," in *Butler's Lives of the Saints: New Full Edition: January*, Revised by Paul Burns, Collegeville, MN: The Liturgical Press/Burns & Oates, 1998, pp. 49-50.
- Jean-Guy Dubuc, *Brother André: Friend of Suffering, Apostle of St. Joseph,* Notre Dame, IN: Ave Maria Press, 2010.

Chapter 53

30th Sunday in Ordinary Time – C
A Prayer When I'm Hated

Scripture:

- Sirach 35: 12-14, 16-18
- Psalm 34: 2-3, 17-18, 19 & 23
- 2 Timothy 4: 6-8, 16-18
- Luke 18: 9-14

Today as we gather to celebrate the Eucharist on this Thirtieth Sunday in Ordinary Time, we hear very clear messages about the Lord's special love for those who suffer at the hands of others. Not only does the Lord especially hear and love those who are downtrodden in society, he despises the self-righteousness that leads others to feel that those people are less worthy in God's sight.

When we read about self-righteous people and how they look down on everyone else, we have to admit that Jesus could just as easily have said this very same thing in 21st-century America. And though we all can identify the self-righteousness that we see everywhere, we don't always try to fight against this evil. But we should, for self-righteousness can lead to destruction of the human spirit, violence, and even death.

One man who sought to do his part against the effects of self-righteousness was Jesuit Father James Martin. He was terribly disturbed by the bullying that led some gay youths to commit suicide. As a result, he wrote a prayer called "A Prayer When I Feel Hated." And though it was designed for sexual minority children and teens, it equally applies to all people in our society who are the victims of hatred, such as prisoners, the homeless, the poor, immigrants, people of color, and people of minority religions. This is Fr. Martin's prayer:

"A Prayer When I Feel Hated"

Loving God, you made me who I am.
I praise you and I love you, for I am wonderfully made,
in your own image.

But when people make fun of me,
I feel hurt and embarrassed and even ashamed.
So please God, help me remember my own goodness,
which lies in you.
Help me remember my dignity,
which you gave me when I was conceived.
Help me remember that I can live a life of love.
Because you created my heart.

Be with me when people make fun of me,
and help me to respond how you would want me to,
in a love that respects others, but also respects me.
Help me find friends who love me for who I am.
Help me, most of all, to be a loving person.

And God, help me remember that Jesus loves me.
For he was seen as an outcast, too.
He was misunderstood, too.
He was beaten and spat upon.
Jesus understands me, and loves me with a special love,
because of the way you made me.

And when I am feeling lonely,
help me remember that Jesus welcomed everyone as a friend.
Jesus reminded everyone that God loved them.
And Jesus encouraged everyone to embrace their dignity,
even when others were blind to that dignity.
Jesus loved everyone with the love that you gave him.
And he loves me, too.

One more thing, God:
Help me remember that nothing is impossible with you,
that you have a way of making things better,
that you can find a way of love for me,
even if I can't see it right now.
Help me remember all these things in the heart you created,
Loving God.
Amen.

This is indeed a powerful prayer that many people could treasure.

But prayer is not enough. We must also search our hearts and minds for seeds of hatred, for it is hate that leads us to disrespect and exclusion and violence. It is hatred that leads us away from Jesus Christ. It is hatred that makes us enemies of Christ's message.

We need to replace any seeds of hatred and its consequences with love, inclusion, respect, and peace. Anything less is unacceptable.

So as we continue our life journeys this week, it would be a good idea to examine our own lives. Are we the self-righteous people that Jesus is condemning in his Gospel message today? If so, what will we change to become people of love?

And that is the good news I have for you on this Thirtieth Sunday in Ordinary Time.

Story source: "A Prayer When I Feel Hated," by Fr. James Martin, S.J., found on WWW in many locations including *Always Catholic.*

Chapter 54

31st Sunday in Ordinary Time – C
Molly & Priesthood Sunday

Scripture:

- Wisdom 11: 22 – 12: 2
- Psalm 145: 1-2, 8-9, 10-11, 13cd-14
- 2 Thessalonians 1: 11 – 2: 2
- Luke 19: 1-10

As we gather to celebrate the Eucharist on this Thirty-First Sunday in Ordinary Time, Catholic Christians throughout the United States celebrate this as Priesthood Sunday. The purpose of Priesthood Sunday is to honor the ordained priesthood, for without it, we could not have the Eucharist.

On this day, we encounter two readings that are very important in discussing the ordained priesthood. The first is from the Book of Wisdom. In this passage, we hear that God has mercy on all, and that God could not hate something that he created. Therefore, all of us are precious and beloved in the eyes of God. This is truly important, because often God calls people whom we often overlook to be leaders of the community. That is what we see in the story of little Zacchaeus, a rich tax collector whom Jesus chose over everyone else to dine in his house.

Unfortunately, though, we often do not see what God sees. We often go through the world with blinders on. We cannot see into the hearts and souls of people all around us. We can even make people invisible. That is what happened to little Molly.

There was once a family who went to a restaurant for dinner one evening. The waiter passed out menus to everyone at the table including eight-year-old Molly. As the only child among the parents and grandparents, Molly felt left out of the adult conversation. When the waiter returned to take orders, he came to Molly last. "And what would you like to have?" the waiter asked Molly.

Molly replied, "I'd like a hot dog and soda."

Molly's grandmother interrupted Molly and said to the waiter, "No, she'll have the roasted chicken, carrots, and mashed potatoes."

The father chimed in, "And she'll have milk, not soda."

As the waiter turned to walk away, he stopped, turned around, and asked Molly, "And would you like mustard or ketchup on your hot dog?"

"Ketchup," Molly replied. Molly then turned to her family and said, "You know what? He thinks I'm real!"

In this story, the waiter, who himself was probably often made invisible by others, was able to see what others could not see: little Molly was real. She was important. She was a child of God.

Now, how does this tie into Priesthood Sunday? Well, if you look around at the men whom God chooses to enter the ordained priesthood, you might be amazed. You can probably name plenty of people whom you think are more "worthy" or "holy" or "qualified."

As an ordained priest, I can name *hundreds* of people whom I think would be excellent priests who were not chosen. But then, I remember, I am not God. I cannot see into the souls and hearts of people like God can do.

So what can the laity do to celebrate the ordained priesthood? Here are just three actions.

First, support seminarians and priests in their rugged vocational journeys. The Knights of Columbus serves as a model in this regard. They pledge to support their parish priests and can always be counted on to pitch in when asked. Furthermore, they support seminarians with prayers, good wishes, and cash gifts. It is little wonder that this group is truly treasured by pastors.

Sometimes, though, people do not support priests. Now before you think that I'm referring to non-Catholic critics, I am not. Rather, I'm referring to people in the Church itself who are continually critical of ordained priests. Seminarians, for example, are often surprisingly critical of priests they encounter. They are convinced that they could do a better job and be much holier and more wonderful. Maybe they could. However, I will never forget a little chat that the seminarians of the Diocese of Cleveland – I was one of them - had with their bishop one evening. We were gathered in a parlor of the seminary. The bishop, knowing how critical seminarians can be of priests, calmly said, "Gentlemen, before you criticize the priests you encounter, remember this: You have not experienced being an ordained priest for even one day of your lives!" Naturally, we seminarians did not want to hear that, but on reflection, I realize it was so very, very true.

Currently there are groups of laity on the Internet who are doing the same thing. They believe that God has called them to serve as judges and declare to the world who are "good" priests and who are "bad" priests. Such people attempt to counteract the loving support that others, such as the Knights, are trying to accomplish.

A second way of supporting ordained priests is by helping in recruitment. Often we are like the people who saw Molly as invisible. We don't recognize people right in front of us who might make fine priests.

For instance, some don't think of asking older men to consider priesthood. By ignoring them, they are making a big mistake: in the United States today, the average age of ordination is forty-three.

And third, pray that Church leaders be open to the Holy Spirit, recognizing God's signs in making policies affecting priesthood.

And that is the good news I have for you on this Thirty-First Sunday in Ordinary Time.

Story source: Anonymous, "I'm Real," in William J. Bausch (Ed.), *A World of Stories for Preachers and Teachers,* Mystic, CT: Twenty-Third Publications, 1998, #262, p. 360.

Chapter 55

32nd Sunday in Ordinary Time – C
Bl. José Luis Sánchez Del Rio

Scripture:

- 2 Maccabees 7: 1-2, 9-14
- Psalm 17: 1, 5-6, 8 & 15
- 2 Thessalonians 2: 16 – 3: 5
- Luke 20: 27-38

As we gather together today to celebrate the Eucharist on this Thirty-Second Sunday in Ordinary Time, we encounter the incredibly inspirational story of a mother and her seven sons who gave their lives rather than renounce their faith.

Sometimes when we read Bible stories like this one, we think to ourselves, "Well, that's a great story, but that was long ago. It couldn't happen today." That kind of thinking, however, is wrong. Not only could it happen today, it does happen in our own times. Just as the Bible story is so inspirational, so is the incredible story of Blessed José Luis Sánchez del Rio.

Of all the Mexican martyrs who gave their lives during the Cristero War (1926-1929), certainly one of the most shining ones was 14-year old José Luis Sánchez del Rio.

José was born on March 28, 1913 in Sahuayo, Michoacán. Later, his family moved to Guadalajara, Jalisco where he attended school.

In 1926, when the Cristero War broke out, José's two brothers joined the rebel Catholic forces to fight against the anti-Catholic laws that were being enforced by the government. Young José very much wanted to join the fight, for he believed that when people are martyred for their faith, they go straight to heaven. However, José's mother, as well as rebel general Prudencio Mendoza, thought he was too young. José pleaded with his mother, "Mama, do not let me lose the opportunity to gain heaven so easily and so soon." Eventually, José's mother and the general gave José permission to join the rebel forces.

The general made José a flag bearer, and the Cristeros nicknamed him Tarcisius after the early Christian saint who gave his life defending the Eucharist.

When the general's horse was killed in battle, José gave his horse to the general. Government soldiers captured José and jailed him in the sacristy of a local church. To break his spirit, they forced him watch the hanging of another Cristero and told him to renounce his faith. José, however, simply encouraged the man to keep the faith and that they would soon meet in heaven. Instead of renouncing the faith, José yelled out the battle cry of the Cristeros, "Viva Cristo Rey!" (Long live Christ the King!).

When the government decided it was time to kill José, they marched him to the cemetery. But before the journey, they cut the bottoms of his feet and forced him to walk barefoot over salt. He was then required to walk barefoot to the cemetery. On that journey, he would sometimes be stopped and given the chance to renounce his Catholic faith. Each time, he would shout, "Viva Cristo Rey!" When he would do this, his captors would slash him with their machetes. Even though he was bleeding and crying, young José refused to renounce his faith or his God.

When José finally made it to the cemetery, his captors gave him one last chance to renounce his faith. José shouted, "I will never give in. Viva Cristo Rey!" The soldiers stabbed him many times with bayonets, but he kept shouting, "Viva Cristo Rey!" That so infuriated the leader that he pulled out a pistol and shot José in the head. As he fell onto the ground, José drew a cross on the ground with his blood, kissed it, and died.

José was declared "Blessed" by Pope Benedict XVI on November 20, 2005. The pope will canonize Blessed José on October 16, 2016. Blessed José Luis Sánchez del Rio's feast day is February 10th, the day of his death.

The story of Blessed José, like the stories of all martyrs, is important in at least three ways.

First, the stories remind us that life on this Earth is not our final destination. So although we should live our lives with full gusto and be engaged with others to the best of our abilities, we should always remember that heaven is our final destination, not earth. That means, of course, that we should not become attached to things of this world.

Pope Benedict XVI reflected on this very thing one day. He pointed out that martyrdom reflects an intense freedom on the part of the martyr. Martyrs are extremely free persons, free from the power of the world.

Second, such stories are sterling examples of the virtue of courage. It's hard to imagine what it must have been like for a fourteen-year old boy to remain faithful in the face of such torture. All he had to do was to renounce Christ, and he would be set free from his captors. José, however, refused to give in. His dying, like his life, reflected courage at its very finest.

And finally, stories of the martyrs remind us that with God's grace, we can accomplish amazing things. As a little boy in Catholic school, I remember hearing the stories of martyrs and being worried. I was concerned that my faith was not great enough, and that if I were ever to face martyrdom, I would not be courageous enough. The Sister who was my teacher said, "Bobby, don't worry. When God calls people to be martyrs, he gives them special graces to endure it."

This week as we continue our life journeys, let's take some time to reflect on our own faith. If God could give us grace to give our very lives for him, will he not give us the graces necessary to meet the much less demanding challenges we have in our lives?

And that is the good news I have for you on this Thirty-Second Sunday in Ordinary Time.

Story source: Several entries on the WWW were used in the story of Blessed José Luís Sánchez del Rio.

Chapter 56

33rd Sunday in Ordinary Time – C
Gossip the Killer

Scripture:

- Malachi 3: 19-20a
- Psalm 98: 5-6, 7-9a, 9bc
- 2 Thessalonians 3: 7-12
- Luke 21: 5-19

As we gather to celebrate the Eucharist on this Thirty-Third Sunday in Ordinary Time, we encounter St. Paul's second letter to the Thessalonians.

In this letter, Paul tells that community that he has heard that many of them have been behaving as "busybodies," meddling in other people's lives instead of minding their own business and working hard.

All of us are familiar with busybodies, for that characteristic is present even today. And frequently these people spread gossip about others. This is a terrible thing, for it can destroy lives.

In the following anonymous essay, we get a glimpse into the spiritual cancer called gossip.

Do You Know Me?

I have no respect for justice. I maim without killing. I break hearts and ruin lives. I am cunning and malicious and gather strength with age.

The more I am quoted, the more I am believed. I flourish at every level of society.

My victims are helpless. They cannot protect themselves against me, for I have no face and no name. To track me down is impossible. The harder you try, the more elusive I become.

I am nobody's friend. Once I tarnish a reputation, it is never quite the same.

I topple governments and wreck marriages. I ruin careers, and cause sleepless nights, heartaches, and grief. I make innocent people cry into their pillow. I make headlines and heartaches.

I am called gossip!

The next time you want to tell a story about someone...think. Is it true? Is it necessary? Is it kind? If not, please don't say it!

This is a very powerful essay, for it reminds us just how damaging gossip can be. For Christians, gossip is wrong on so many levels, for it violates both the Hebrew commandments that we treasure, and also the Christian commandments of love.

When we seek to harm another person with our speech, we violate at least three of the ten Hebrew commandments. First, the Fifth Commandment: "You shall not kill." Killing is far more than simply destroying one's body. We can kill another's spirit by our harmful rhetoric. We can kill the spirit, and damage mental and physical health, with harmful stories about another person. This can, as we have recently seen in cyber-bullying, lead to suicide.

Second, harming others by our speech violates the Seventh Commandment, "You shall not steal." When we tell bad things about another, we rob them of their good name. We steal their reputations. Once a reputation is damaged, it is nearly impossible to repair completely.

And finally, when we tell bad things about another, we violate the Eighth Commandment - "You shall not bear false witness against your neighbor." But, you might say, what if the thing I am saying against my neighbor is true? It doesn't matter. If your words are designed to harm another person, whether true or false, you have violated this commandment.

In addition to violating the Hebrew commandments, deliberately harming others by our talk is a violation of the basic law of our Christian faith, the triple love commandment of Jesus. Specifically, it violates the law of loving one's neighbor.

Spreading gossip is an incredibly difficult thing to combat, for it is so very delicious. Many people thrive on the misfortunes and misbehaviors of others. They live to gossip just as birds live to fly and fish live to swim. To harm others with their tongues is an obsession with them.

Amazingly, such people often see themselves as paragons of virtue. In fact, many of them see themselves as morally superior to others. Telling about others' faults reinforces, in their minds, how noble and virtuous they themselves are. They are like the hypocrites that Jesus condemned in so many ways on so many occasions.

As we continue our life journeys this week, maybe it would be a good idea to examine our lives. How do I spread gossip? How do I violate the Hebrew and Christian commandments by harming others' reputations? How can I be a more loving person?

And that is the good news I have for you on this Thirty-Third Sunday in Ordinary Time.

Story source: Anonymous, "Do You Know Me?" in Brian Cavanaugh (Ed.), *Fresh Packet of Sower's Seeds: Third Planting,* New York: Paulist Press, 1994, #90, p. 80.

Chapter 57

Christ the King – C
Come Unto Me

Scripture:

- 2 Samuel 5: 1-3
- Psalm 122: 1-2, 3-4ab, 4cd-5
- Colossians 1: 12-20
- Luke 23: 35-43

Today the Catholic Church celebrates the final Sunday of the church year with the Feast of Christ the King. At the end of this week, we'll end Year C, the year of Luke, and enter Year A, the year of Matthew.

Pope Pius XI instituted the feast of Christ the King in 1925 to remind Christians that Jesus Christ reigns over all creation. He declared this feast to counteract the forces of atheism and secularism of his day. For Catholic Christians, this day also reminds us that all human beings are our brothers and sisters. Therefore, we should never get caught up in "nationalism," a belief that sometimes leads people to put their love of country before their love of their Catholic faith.

The idea of Christ as a "king" is one of many images that Christians have of Jesus. For some, it is a very helpful image, but for others, it is not so helpful. That is exactly what the sculptor in the following story learned.

There was once a famous sculptor who decided one day that he would create the greatest statue of Jesus ever made in the history of the world. In his mind, the best way to portray Jesus Christ was as a king, a strong, dominant, regal type of figure.

And that is exactly what he did at his seaside studio. When he finished his masterpiece, he looked at it carefully. It was indeed a marvel to behold: a strong, masculine, almost fierce figure. He said to himself, "This is indeed the best work I have ever done."

During the night, however, a heavy fog rolled into the area, and sea spray came in through an open window, affecting the shape of the clay.

When the sculptor returned to his studio in the morning, he was shocked. Droplets of moisture had formed on the model, creating the illusion of bleeding. The head of the statue drooped. The stern-looking face now became one of compassion. And the arms that had once been raised as a triumphant king now drooped down into a posture of welcome. The statue now looked like a wounded Christ-figure.

The sculptor was at first devastated. He imagined that he would have to start all over again. But the more he looked at the new look of the statue, the more he came to like it. In fact, he realized that the new image was a much truer visualization of Christ than the one he had created. He realized that God had sent the fog and the sea spray deliberately. So, he carved these words into the base of the new statue: *Come unto me.*

The sculptor realized that the kingly figure that he originally had created did not reflect the actual Jesus who lived on this planet. Jesus lived a simple life, coming from a small village, born in a stable beside animals. He grew up to be a storyteller who continually took the side of the poor and the weak and the outcasts of society. Instead of focusing on the letter of the Jewish law, he focused instead on the spirit of the law. He was forever preaching compassion, love, mercy, and forgiveness.

The story of the sculptor, the Gospel selection we have today from Luke, and the Church's creation of this Feast of Christ the King can teach us at least three things.

First, as Christians, we should live a Christ-centered life. We live Christ-centered lives when we imitate Christ in our daily lives. That means we seek to see the Christ who lives in every person and treat that person accordingly. That means we continually strive to find the good in everyone. It means we are always ready to show mercy instead of calling for punishment. It means giving others the benefit of the doubt and giving others a second chance. It means living our vocations to the best of our ability. It means sharing the good news of Jesus Christ with others, without offending them by overdoing it. It means being people of extraordinary generosity toward those who have less than us. It means striving to rid the gardens of our souls of the weeds of vice and replacing them with the flowers of virtues.

Second, the feast reminds us to adore Jesus Christ as God—God the Son to be exact. No human being should ever come ahead of Christ in our lives. We must never claim allegiance to human-made entities such as nations or political parties when to do so would dilute our allegiance to Christ and His triple love commandment of loving God, neighbor, and self. In other words, we must never make idols out of human leaders, money, power, prestige, material goods, flags, and the like.

Finally, because Jesus Christ is fully human and fully divine, how He can be seen is infinitely complex. Today, for example, the Church celebrates Jesus as the Head of the Church and the whole of creation. But we can't take just one dimension of Jesus and claim that it is "the one way" to see Him. There are many other ways to see Jesus. We can see him as the Good Shepherd, always looking out for the flock. We can see him as the Sacred Heart whose love knows no limits. We can see Him as the

Christ Child, spectacular in humility and simplicity. We can see him as the Teacher, always giving us wisdom. And we can see Him as the Gospel today portrays him, the victim of the death penalty whose last act on Earth was to promise eternal salvation to a criminal.

As we continue our life journeys this week, it would be a good idea to take some time to examine how we see Jesus. What is our favorite image of him? How does that influence how we pray to him?

And that is the good news I have for you on this last Sunday of the Church Year.

Story source: Anonymous, "Come Unto Me," in Brian Cavanaugh (Ed.), *Fresh Packet of Sower's Seeds: Third Planting,* New York: Paulist Press, 1994, #86, p. 78.

37502543R00151

Made in the USA
San Bernardino, CA
20 August 2016